HOW TO LEAD A WEIGHT LOSS SUPPORT GROUP

The Kosloff Method

Five comprehensive meetings, including tips, exercises, recipes, and a menu plan based on the Mediterranean diet

Yaffa Kosloff

The information and menus in this book are not intended to replace professional medical advice. Before starting this or any weight-loss program, consult with your physician, and continue to be monitored by your physician while you are losing weight.

Published by

KTAV PUBLISHING HOUSE

527 Empire Blvd

Brooklyn, NY 11225

www.ktav.com

orders@ktav.com

Ph: (718) 972-5449

5 Shahar St.

Jerusalem Israel 9626307

https://ykosloff.com/en/

yafak@yahoo.com

Book and cover design by Maya Enov
Cover photograph by Mariana Stebeneva
Cover photograph, seating from left to right: Ariana Zakes, Ayelet Stain (Ayelet lost 33 pounds with the Kosloff method), Sonya Enov, Yaffa Kosloff, Josh Frankenhuis (Josh lost 59 pounds with the Kosloff Method), Rozit Frankenhuis, Olga Balashov.

Printed in the U.S.A.

ISBN 978-1-60280-388-6

To Ronnie

Contents

Meeting 2

Meeting 3

Meeting 4

Meeting 5

Appendix

Intro

Foreword

Leading weight-loss groups is such a rewarding career!

Helping a person transform in the ways she desires. Watching a person become happier and more beautiful, like a flower reaching its peak bloom. Earning an income and endless gratitude for your work as a group leader.

I can't think of a better career in the world. This book is the first and only guidebook that teaches you how to lead a weight-loss support group.

Is it your dream to have an exciting, satisfying career that can help you control your weight? This book you are holding is the first step toward realizing that dream. I accompany you every step of the way, and in turn you will help others realize their dreams.

How it all started

Up until the age of 42 I was overweight – I was a chubby baby, a plump little girl, a heavy teenager, a fat college student, and an overweight young mom. At the early age of 12, I began to seek out diets. I would desperately attempt any diet I heard about, even the most extreme fads. Always motivated at the beginning, I would follow the diet to a tee, losing 6 to 8 pounds (3 to 4 kilos) within the first few weeks only to fall off the dieting wagon and eat everything

in sight. At the end of these binges, I found I had regained all my weight and then some.

This cycle of losing and gaining weight affected how I felt about myself and my abilities. It ate away my self-esteem. With my extra weight, I was embarrassed to leave the house and go out with friends.

I wanted to be thin so badly that I bought into all sorts of scams, even a pair of pants that supposedly made you sweat and lose weight. I even dreamed about having intestinal parasites.

It all started by chance. After the birth of my third son 30 years ago, I was 35 pounds overweight. An idea came to me – perhaps I could have more success dieting with the support of a group. I gathered some friends who shared my same struggles, and we agreed to meet once a week at my home. Every meeting I would hand out a weekly menu, and the group would weigh in, share ideas about how to overcome temptations, and mostly laugh a lot. We all lost weight. Evidently, the sense of warmth, the small-group atmosphere, and the mutual support helped us achieve our weight-loss goals and keep the weight off long-term.

Without any advertising at all, friends of friends approached me to ask if I would start a new weight-loss group. I hesitated at first, but eventually agreed. The word got out that there was a group where everyone successfully lost weight, where the leader called if you missed a meeting, and where people noticed if you had a bad week and needed encouragement.

There was demand to start more and more groups.

But the path to success was anything but simple. It frightens me today to think about how I began leading the first weight-loss group without any understanding of how people make changes in their lives or which weight-loss menus can be followed in the long run.

My method developed through trial and error. If I had only gotten ahold of this book, I would have spared myself many mistakes!

Our menu is based on the Mediterranean diet, which emphasizes large quantities of vegetables for breakfast, lunch, and dinner. The menu has been altered many times throughout the years, according to the groups' outcomes. I removed fruit salad, rice, and quinoa from the menu after I saw that participants didn't lose weight during the weeks these foods were included. Since the majority of my clients are working women, I put a lot of effort into ensuring that meal preparation would be simple and time efficient.

Over the years, I read all the self-help books I could get my hands on, and these books helped me to create the meeting syllabi. Group participants also contributed wonderful ideas that appear in many of these syllabi.

I developed exercises that helped participants stay motivated after the meeting and maintain healthy eating habits during the week. And I spent a lot of time pondering over questions like "what inspires people to make changes in their lives?", "what motivates participants to attend every meeting?", and "how can meetings become interesting for participants, or even make them laugh?"

Not all meeting syllabi stuck with me over the years. But if participants lost weight the week after our meeting, I always kept that syllabus.

I learned not to allow people to join a group after the first meeting because only in this way could we create a warm environment that enabled mutual trust and support.

I learned that I have to stop participants from sharing and focusing on their failures, after a particularly dominant woman went on and on about the frozen cookies she ate straight from the freezer. This woman didn't lose any weight, and her group's achievements were especially low as well.

I summarized all the important principles I discovered during my 30 years of leading weight-loss groups and included the syllabi for the first five weeks (the most important) in this book.

Your desire to support others and maintain your own weight led you to buy this book and read it up to this point. All that's left is to start your first group.

Don't hesitate - just do it!

Best Wishes,

Yaffa Kosloff

THE NUMBERS SPEAK FOR THEMSELVES

- **30 years** of leading weight-loss groups
- **80,000** excess pounds shed thanks to the Kosloff Method
- **6-month** waitlist to join a group
- **180-pound** individual record for weight loss in a group
- **50%** of participants who lost weight using my method have maintained their weight long-term
- **15 leaders** using the Kosloff Method

How to use this book

The five meeting descriptions in this book are written in the spoken language participants would hear in my weight-loss group and contain everything said aloud during the first five sessions.

Read the meeting description and accompanying tips thoroughly before conducting each of your own meetings. Summarize the content for yourself and outline it using the section titles.

Each of the five meetings includes an exercise and menu.

It is important to read all of the book's addendums before your first meeting, in order to understand certain ideas developed throughout the book. (For example, what is the secret contract between the leader and group participants?) You will also get important tips like how to download printer-friendly versions of the exercises and menus from our website and how to adapt the menu for participants who require more calories.

This hourglass symbolizes reaction time. The icon means: "Now give the group time to think, react and brainstorm."

Meeting 1

Private weigh-in

At the first meeting, I weigh each participant, write down her weight on a pre-prepared card, and sincerely wish her success with a big smile.

Getting to know you

Hello, good evening. Everybody in this room is here to lose weight and to learn to eat healthy.

To successfully lose weight, you must do five simple things, nothing complicated, that each and every one of you is capable of doing. Before getting into these five things, let's start with a quick "getting to know you"

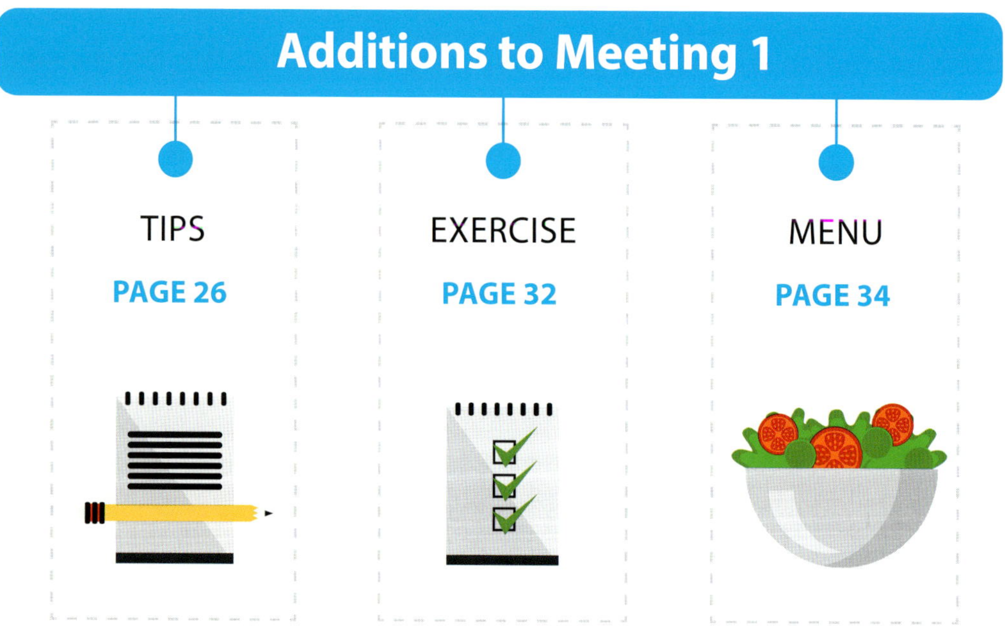

exercise that will help us get better acquainted with each other. Tell us your name and the main reason you want to lose weight. Take a minute to think. Introduce yourself and finish the following sentence: "I want to lose weight because..."

Afterwards I introduce myself, trying not to be overly humble. I like to mention that I am not a dietician and that I actually have a bachelor degree in statistics and a master's degree in economics. Finally, I describe my long journey to the Kosloff weight-loss method. As a group leader, be sure to share positive things about yourself. Talk about the days when you were overweight and unsuccessfully tried to lose weight, to build the participants' connection with you.

Five rules for dieting success

Anyone who decides to join our group must embrace the following five rules for success.

Point to the five fingers on your hand.

Rule 1

ATTEND EVERY MEETING

Actively participating in our support groups creates magic. **People have an exceptional ability to change when they are part of a group.** We're inspired to successfully change behaviors because everyone is working towards one common goal. To be part of this magic, attend each and every meeting.

Knowing without question that you'll be weighed every week at the mandatory meetings will definitely affect the way you eat. Before reaching for a cookie, you'll tell yourself, "Am I crazy? I'm going to be weighed in three days!"

Anyone who cannot attend a meeting during the first month should schedule a private appointment with me to make up the missed meeting.

2

Rule 2

EAT HEALTHY, ENJOYABLE, CALMING, AND SATISFYING FOODS

Hunger is the biggest enemy of weight loss.

Our strongest natural impulse is to eat when we're hungry.

What types of food should you eat to lose weight without starving yourself? ⌛

Lots of vegetables. There is no better trick for losing weight. Eating lots of vegetables allows us to maintain weight loss over a long period of time by feeling satiated, without our stomachs grumbling even once throughout the day. Our diet includes quiches, roasted or stir-fried vegetables, and terrific salads. This is what I call **feel-good** food. Why does this food make us feel good? Precisely because it is delicious when we it eat it, and an hour later a pleasant and relaxed feeling still lingers. Our behavior makes us feel good emotionally, and nourishing our bodies with healthy, calming, and satisfying food makes us feel good physically.

By preparing meals from the recipe sheets, you'll discover which vegetable recipes you like most, and these will likely stay with you for a lifetime. Each week you will receive some new vegetable recipes, which generally have enough servings to last for several days. Preparing all of the recipes should take about 15 minutes a day. However, it is possible to lose weight even if you invest less time in preparation. Take half a bag of prewashed, ready-to-eat salad, place it in a nice bowl, add 10 cherry tomatoes, season with salt, pepper, and olive oil, and top it with 7 ounces (200 g) of protein such as chicken, fish, or cheese. An easy and delicious dietetic meal that only takes five minutes to prepare!

3 Rule 3

DO NOT SKIP ANY MEALS

If I were to pass out a questionnaire to all of you sitting here, asking you about your eating habits, we would learn that almost everyone eats the same way. In the morning, we don't eat anything because we're rushing and we don't feel hungry. Later at work we're too busy to feel hungry so we either eat a light snack or nothing at all. The thought even crosses our minds, "Wow, amazing! I'm losing weight." Yet as soon as we walk through the door at home, we start eating everything in sight. We eat a ton, first savory then sweet, but nothing calms our hunger. We find ourselves hungry over and over again for savory then sweet foods. Instead of losing weight, we find that we've actually gained a pound in a month.

Why do we gain weight eating this way? ⌛

The body has its own mind, called the primitive brain, which controls many physical processes. For example, when we eat something spoiled, the body's primitive brain causes stomach cramping that triggers vomiting. When we barely eat during the day, the primitive brain thinks we're on the verge of dying of starvation.

What are you in the mood to eat after a long day? Do you feel like eating a salad or something else? ⌛

If you barely eat anything all day, the primitive brain triggers cravings for high-calorie foods and fast! You will have a strong desire to eat fried foods or processed foods high in fat, such as pizza, take-out food, or sugary foods like chocolate and cake.

When there is a conflict between the rational brain that desires weight loss and the primitive brain of our stomach, who wins? ⌛

The primitive brain always wins!

What can we do? Do not skip any meals.

There are five daily meals:

1. **Breakfast,** which you should eat soon after waking up.
2. **10 a.m. light meal**
3. **Lunch**
4. **4 p.m. light meal**
5. **Dinner**

After eating throughout the day, we arrive home relaxed, full of the patience and energy we need to prepare ourselves a healthy meal.

Sitting down to a meal that consists of protein and salad, we enjoy every bite. We think to ourselves, "Why don't I always eat salad? It's so delicious!" The reason you've never wanted to eat salad is that you've been too hungry.

Remember: there is a direct connection between skipping meals during the day and overeating.

At work, we are faced with other challenges. A fellow employee has a birthday and at 3:00 in the afternoon a 16-layer, 1000-calorie piece of cake descends

unexpectedly onto your desk. If you haven't eaten much, all the self-control in the world won't help. You'll devour the entire piece.

Come evening, do you even remember that piece of cake? ⌛

Yes, you'll swear that you haven't had anything to eat since the morning. Who remembers a piece of cake gobbled down in a second that only left a craving for more?

Your behavior is entirely different if you have already eaten breakfast, a 10 a.m. light meal, and lunch by the time the cake arrives at your desk. Your personality has changed. You demonstrate self-control, telling yourself, "I'll never put this trans-fat infused junk into my body." After tossing the cake in the garbage, and hiding it under a few papers, you pull out the sandwich or apple you brought from home as a wonderful feeling of control washes over you. Nothing could be sweeter than this victory.

Rule 4

EXERCISES FOR CHANGING THOUGHT PATTERNS

Each week you will be asked to practice a daily one- to five-minute exercise. These exercises are so simple that some people think they cannot possibly be effective. Even if the exercise sounds silly, please do it. You'll discover how it influences the behaviors you want to change. But it's impossible to discover how the exercise influences you without trying it. Coming to the group without practicing the simple exercises is like being accepted to the Basketball Champion League and refusing to practice shooting.

Rule 5

30 MINUTES OF DAILY EXERCISE OR WALKING

Research on people who lost weight and managed to keep it off show that these people added daily exercise to their schedule. Yes, **every day.**

Why does exercise help with weight loss? ⌛

Physical activity has many helpful benefits for weight loss and maintaining your new weight.

Your body burns calories during exercise and continues to burn them at rest because your metabolism improves. Exercising keeps you out of the kitchen and away from food. High-intensity exercise releases endorphins that make you feel good. After high-intensity exercise, hunger is decreased for half an hour.

If you already exercise for an hour every day, that's enough. However, if you exercise twice a week, you should add half an hour of walking on the other days.

If you have a physical limitation that makes walking difficult, you can do 10 minutes of seated exercise three times a day. Another option is walking for 15 minutes twice a day. Thirty-minute workout classes can be found on the internet, such as Pilates, yoga, or another type of moderate exercise. Incorporate walking into your daily routine. Just as you would never skip brushing your teeth before bed, even if you're dead tired, never ever skip your daily walk.

The leader's commitment

Anyone who shows up at the next meeting is essentially announcing to herself, the leader, and the entire group that she agrees to the five rules: attend all group meetings, prepare vegetable dishes, eat all of the daily meals, practice the simple exercises, and walk at least 30 minutes a day.

As the group leader, I promise that anyone who follows all five of these rules **will lose weight and learn to eat healthy**. I promise to be available for phone consultations when you encounter difficulties. I promise to provide support and encouragement from beginning to end, until you reach your goal.

Payment: *Now it's time to talk about membership fees. Yes, I know talking about money is awkward, but we have to talk about the price for joining the group.*

Weekly Exercise

FINDING YOUR FEEL-GOOD FOOD

The simple exercise for this week is to write down everything you eat, the time you eat it, and how you feel afterwards.

Weight loss is certainly our goal. However, in order to keep the pounds off we have to learn to eat feel-good foods. What is a feel-good food? Definitely not some sugary treat that leaves you craving for more and feeling unsatisfied. Rather, it's delicious food that even an hour later leaves us free from thinking about eating, thanks to the pleasant and relaxing feeling in our bodies.

Writing down what you eat creates self-awareness about hunger, satiation, and feelings of relaxation. Hopefully you won't deviate from the menu, but if you do, make note of this too. Likewise, write down whether or not you enjoyed each meal. Every person enjoys different foods from the menu. You can only know if the meal left you feeling hungry or satiated after an hour, because sometimes feelings of satiation come much later.

Clarifying menu topics

Do not hand out the menu yet.

UNLIMITED VEGETABLES

All vegetables are "free" on our diet, meaning that you can eat as much as you want, except for potatoes, sweet potatoes, peas, avocado, and corn, which are not considered vegetables.

You can always prepare a salad or vegetable soup as an extra boost when you feel hungry. Since all vegetables are unlimited, if the menu lists a tomato and cucumber salad, you can certainly prepare a cabbage and carrot salad or any other salad instead.

CARB DETOX

Some of you may be eating lots of carbohydrates every day, such as sugary snacks or cake or lots of bread, or...? ⌛

Wait for the group to add other carbs and then fill in pasta, potatoes, and even fruit.

You might experience withdrawal symptoms for two days. Detoxing from carbs is not like detoxing from hard drugs. But it is common to have a light headache or dizziness during the first two days. Or you might feel terrific. If you have a headache or feel dizzy, eat a few cherry tomatoes because these also contain

carbohydrates and can calm you down a bit. Everything will be easier after the first two days.

CAFFEINE

Whoever generally drinks several cups of coffee with milk will notice that there is no milk included in the diet plan. Next week I will give a detailed explanation of why and how much is allowed, but for now you can add 1 tablespoon of milk to each cup of coffee, up to 4 tablespoons a day. Measure them exactly. If you are used to drinking a lot of coffee, you are addicted to your daily caffeine intake. Withdrawal symptoms from caffeine are much stronger than those from carbohydrates: intense migraines, dizziness, fatigue, and a general feeling of unwellness. Since we don't want people detoxing from carbs and caffeine in the same week, add 1 cup of strong black coffee, without milk, for every 2 cups of Nescafé that you eliminate.

LIGHT BREAD

The first ingredient listed on the light bread you choose should be whole wheat flour. The number of calories per slice must be no more than 45. Light bread is made from flour that contains more protein, making it easier to slice into thinner and airier pieces and also more satiating. If you cannot find light bread where you live, substitute one slice of light bread with half a slice of whole wheat bread containing up to 90 calories. Likewise, if you avoid gluten and eat other types of flour, you should eat half a slice instead of one slice of light bread.

All bread substitutes, such as crackers and rice cakes, do not satiate at all, so do not eat these on the diet.

TWO SANDWICHES

If you regularly come home from work after 3 p.m., you will have to eat lunch on the go because otherwise you'll come home famished. Two sandwiches made

with light bread are the perfect substitute for lunch, which can be conveniently eaten at work or while travelling. The sandwiches don't have to be measly – on the contrary, they should be feel-good and satisfying. Each sandwich can be filled with 50 calories: two slices of cold cuts, or one slice of feta cheese, or a spoon of cottage cheese, or half an egg, or a quarter avocado. Add lettuce or arugula leaves, radishes, cucumbers, or any other vegetable.

It is mandatory to eat at least four vegetables in addition to the sandwiches. Alternating between one bite of sandwich and two bites of vegetables, you'll be satiated. Men can fill each sandwich with 100 calories.

GETTING READY FOR A LONG DAY

If you leave the house early in the morning for the entire day and you have to drop off your kids at school or daycare, don't fool yourself into thinking you'll be able to successfully prepare your food in the morning. Before going to bed, prepare food for the next day and leave it in the refrigerator, including breakfast, lunch, and the 10 a.m. and 4 p.m. light meals. An entire bag of food! In the morning, just grab the bag before leaving the house.

MENU

Now it's time to hand out the menu sheets.

You may choose one day out of the menu plan and use it for the entire week. Next week, there will be more daily diet options to choose from.

Any questions? ⌛

It is important to explain all the instructions before allowing members to ask questions. If anyone has a question, just say, "questions at the end."

Generally there is not enough time for all of the questions, so I ask participants to call me during the week to discuss them over the phone. Make sure to end the meeting on time, as respect for other people's schedules is appreciated.

Some of the participants have likely promised to be home by a certain time.

It's also not a good idea to answer questions about particularly specific problems.Just smile and say, "Let's talk about this problem tomorrow over the phone." Write down the person's name so they'll understand that you really intend to call.

Farewell at the end of the meeting

Let's say you decide to learn Italian because you plan to travel to Italy for a month next year and you really want to speak Italian fluently. You sign up for an intensive Italian course that meets four times a week, with an extra two hours of homework after each class. The course progresses quickly, so you can't miss any classes. Whoever makes this huge investment in studying Italian will be able to speak fluently within a year. Clearly, if this is your dream it can definitely be fulfilled, but only after a lot of hard work. The weight-loss journey and the process of learning new eating habits are just like learning a foreign language. There are thousands of simple tricks to learn in our group – that's why it's so important not to skip any meetings. You will have to invest an hour a day in practicing the exercises, preparing food, and walking. Just like an Italian student, whoever puts in the effort will succeed. Losing weight is a dream that can definitely be fulfilled.

I promise you all that anyone who invests this hour every day will successfully lose weight.

Best of luck to everybody!

Week 1 Tips

What to bring to Meeting 1

1 | Personal weight log for each participant

2 | Medical liability form

3 | Exercise – three log sheets for each participant

4 | Week 1 menu for each patricipant

5 | Your summary of the meeting's content

6 | Pens or pencils

To download the exercise and the menu please go to the chapter: How to print the exercises and menus in a print friendly version for free :)

How to motivate during Week 1

Personal attention makes our group different from others. The day after the first meeting, I start calling group members. **I call everybody during the first week** to ask them how it's going and if they have any questions. The most overweight members, who will definitely find the new menu difficult, get a call the very next afternoon. This is often when they almost lose control, and the call keeps them on course.

The call has a few goals:

- To answer specific questions about the diet.
- To motivate members if difficulties arise. If a member has been getting

headaches, ask whether or not she reduced her coffee intake. Be sure to mention that the headache will only last for two days and then the pain will subside. If a member has followed the diet but overeaten a little, I encourage her to continue. On the other hand, if someone hasn't followed the recipes, eaten the daily meals, written down what she ate, or walked, I advise her to make an effort to stick to the diet plan over the next few days. **If she fails to make the effort, she shouldn't attend the next meeting.** Someone who doesn't change any behaviors during the first week will not change habits later on. She may think this was a special week (her mother-in-law was sick, she had to work extra hours), but it will soon become clear that every week is a special week.

Telephone calls – I emphasize at the meeting that I like it when people call or WhatsApp me, and I let them know the best times to call. Everybody is welcome to call with problems big and small. I say something like the following: "Even if you are at the supermarket debating whether or not to buy a certain product, call me. And it goes without saying that you should call me in the middle of crisis. I can't always answer the phone, but leave a message and I'll call you back as soon as possible."

Extra Topic

THE PROJECT

I know that the majority of you work and are busy 16 hours a day – that you've done the math and realize this project will take almost an hour a day. You're probably saying to yourselves, has this lady Yaffa Kosloff gone crazy? Where does she think I'll get an extra hour every day? Who does this grueling diet? My answer is that **if you stick to the diet, the extra hour will create itself.** You will be more energetic, refreshed, and focused throughout the day. You'll need less sleep because as soon as your head hits the pillow you'll fall into a wonderfully deep slumber. The best part is I'm not talking about something that will happen in the distant future after you've lost 40 pounds. You will feel wonderful within just one week.

Please don't leave today with the impression that this diet isn't for you. Decide now to stick to it for one week. If you follow the diet for one week, you'll be pleasantly surprised to see all kinds of positive changes in your life. You'll feel energetic and relaxed, but most importantly, you'll be convinced that it really isn't that complicated to follow the diet. Some of the things you were so worried about will simply go away by themselves.

I wish you all the best of luck and remind you that I'm always here for you.

Learn from my experience

ANSWERING QUESTIONS

At the first meeting, there are usually some participants who have tried many diets in the past. They know that green olives are not vegetables, and it's boring for them to listen to all of the questions. On the other hand, there are some participants who have never been on a diet before. Everything is new, complex, and complicated to them, and they can't absorb all the information. In order to accommodate both audiences, it is important that the lecture be uninterrupted. Leave about 15 minutes at the end of the meeting for questions and ask anyone who still has questions to call you.

Answers to frequently asked questions can be found on the menu as well as on our website: **www.ykosloff.com/en**

SUBSTITUTIONS

In the first groups I led, I was really nice and agreeable, and I allowed members to substitute foods upon request. A 17-year-old girl named Michelle told me she ate cereal every morning. She explained that she would only eat half a cup of cereal with water on the diet. I made some quick calculations and approved the substitution. Michelle didn't lose any weight. The story of failure to lose weight with substitutions repeated itself many times. I learned my lesson the hard way and at the members' expense: someone who starts the day with some cereal, a small cookie, or a cup of orange juice will not lose weight.

As a leader, you will be asked to approve substitutions: a whole-wheat cracker, rice cake, or some cereal instead of the light bread. Members will ask to replace an apple with a peach or plum, or a slice of bread and jam for the 4 p.m. meal.

Remember, the customer paid money to lose weight – don't give in to the customer's cravings!

The answer to all substitution requests is NO! But promise that they'll be able to substitute foods in the future. I tell them to ask again at the tenth meeting, but in the meantime the answer is no.

It is important to promise that these foods will not vanish altogether. Calm them down by saying that we're just eliminating some foods for 10 weeks. Your goal as a leader is to have them stick to the diet perfectly during the first two months. Only someone who eats our tailor-made, satisfying, and calming meals for two whole months can understand the calmness, happiness, and satiety resulting from this exacting diet. Members will feel their cravings for sweets gradually diminish as the days pass. The more precisely a member follows the diet, the easier it is to keep sticking to it.

Medical Liability

Our diet is healthy, good, and balanced, but I do not want to be liable if the participant has a medical problem that requires a different diet. At the first meeting, I immediately have each person sign a form which states:

I am aware that this diet, like any other diet, must be carried out after consultation with my doctor. At the bottom of the page, there is a place for the participant to fill in her name, email address, signature, and the date.

Story Time

THE ANGRY PARTICIPANT

A few years ago, a nice-looking and put-together woman named Liz came to one of my groups. Toward the end of the first meeting, I handed out the menu sheets. Liz briefly looked over the menu and then angrily burst out, "There is nothing to eat here, this is total starvation, I never eat breakfast, I barely have time to drink a cup of coffee. Besides, how will I survive without dessert on the weekend…"

I waited patiently until her outburst was over. Wiping my glasses, I smiled nicely at Liz and the group, took a deep breath, and finally told them: "Liz said something important. In fact, Liz did us a huge favor by voicing the concerns shared by so many others in the group. Liz is afraid of failure. She's afraid the process will be too hard. Apparently she has had lots of bad experiences with diets in the past and has lost a lot of money on those diets. Her anger also comes from the fact that she doesn't want to make changes and give up the foods she loves. Next week, if she attends, Liz will be calmer and nicer. If she follows our healthy eating plan for one week, she will see that the menu is very satiating and she will not be starving all the time. Also, her weekend won't be ruined without dessert."

Liz did come to the second meeting. After this extremely unpleasant start, it was surprising to see Liz be so nice and supportive during the group meetings. It was as if she had become a different person. Liz regularly attended meetings for six months, lost 30 pounds, and looked fabulous. At least 20 members joined my groups afterwards thanks to Liz's warm recommendations.

At the first meeting it is normal for one of the participants to get angry.

She will complain in unpleasant tones: the group is too big, the room is uncomfortable, the diet is unhealthy, there's too much protein included in the diet, there's not enough protein, etc.

Trying to understand this angry participant allows you to remain calm. The person in question is terrified of the diet. She is so afraid of failure that she is anxiously trying to find a serious reason to drop out.

Most importantly, do not get irritated and do not by any means try to justify and explain the amount of protein or the problematic room. Referring to the problems the participant raises will not calm her fears. You can reassure her that many people feel this way at the first meeting and nevertheless succeed and enjoy the group.

Occasionally during this first meeting, there is someone who demands that I adapt the diet to something essential in her life, such as eating cake every night. I answer, "if you do not change your eating habits, your weight will not change."

Week 1 Exercise

WEEKLY FOOD DIARY

JUST FOR TODAY	Day 1	Day 2	Day 3	Day 4	Day 5	Day 6	Day 7
Morning							
10.00							
Noon							

16.00							
Evening							
Exercise Walking, swimming, yoga, pilates							
Drink 8 glasses of water							

Don't skip meals ♡ Find your feel-good foods ♡ Exercise every day

Week 1 Menu

WRITE DOWN EVERYTHING YOU EAT &
HOW YOU FEEL AN HOUR LATER

DAY 1

sport ✓

BREAKFAST	♡ Beverage: coffee, tea, water ♡ 2 slices of light bread ♡ 2 tablespoons 2% low-fat cottage cheese ♡ Tomato and cucumber slices
10:00 AM	♡ Beverage and yogurt
LUNCH	♡ Beverage: coffee, tea, water ♡ 1 slice of light bread ♡ Greek salad from the island of Cyprus (recipe included)
16:00 PM	♡ Beverage and apple
DINNER	♡ 1 slice of light bread ♡ Maya's salad (recipe included) ♡ 3 ounces of tuna fish (80g) or 1 egg

DAYS 2, 3

sport ✓

BREAKFAST	♡ Beverage: coffee, tea, water ♡ Red pepper and arugula ♡ 2 slices of light bread ♡ 2 tablespoons 2% low-fat cottage cheese
10:00 AM	♡ Beverage and yogurt
LUNCH	♡ Beverage: coffee, tea, water ♡ Kosloff cauliflower salad (recipe included) ♡ 1 slice of light bread
16:00 PM	♡ Beverage and apple
DINNER	♡ Honey-mustard salmon or chicken breast (recipe included) ♡ Oven-roasted green beans (recipe included)

DAYS 4, 5		sport
BREAKFAST	♡ Beverage: coffee, tea, water	
	♡ 2 slices of light bread	
	♡ 2 tablespoons 2% low-fat cottage cheese	
	♡ Tomato and cucumber slices	
10:00 AM	♡ Beverage and yogurt	
LUNCH	♡ Beverage: coffee, tea, water	
	♡ Radish, corn, and walnut salad (recipe included)	
	♡ 1 slice of light bread	
16:00 PM	♡ Beverage and apple	
DINNER	♡ 1 thigh or 2 drumsticks of lean chicken (cooked without skin)	
	♡ Pepper delicacy (recipe included)	
	♡ Vegetable salad	

DAYS 6, 7		sport
BREAKFAST	♡ Beverage: coffee, tea, water	
	♡ Omelette made with 1 egg and 1 teaspoon oil	
	♡ 1 slice of light bread	
	♡ Tomato and cucumber slices	
10:00 AM	♡ Beverage and yogurt	
LUNCH	♡ Beverage: coffee, tea, water	
	♡ 3 ounces of tuna fish (80g)	
	♡ Maya's salad (recipe included)	
	♡ 1 slice of light bread	
16:00 PM	♡ Beverage and apple	
DINNER	♡ Oven-roasted green beans (recipe included)	
	♡ 5 ounces (150g) chicken breast or turkey breast	
	♡ 1 slice of light bread	

♥ Snack on fresh vegetable sticks and cherry tomatoes between meals ♥ Eat up to 2 cups of vegetable soup per day ♥ Lunch and dinner can be switched ♥ Drink beverages without added milk or sugar ♥ Eat at least 2 cups of vegetables at lunch and again at dinner ♥ One tablespoon of oil per day is mandatory ♥ During the first week ONLY, you may add 2 slices of light bread per day ♥

Recipes

Greek salad from the island of Cyprus

I AM IN LOVE WITH THIS SALAD

| ONE SERVING

INGREDIENTS

- 2 tomatoes
- 3 cucumbers
- 1/2 yellow pepper
- 4 black olives
- 3 ounces (80g) of 5% feta cheese, cubed

DRESSING

- 1 tablespoon oil
- 1 tablespoon lemon juice
- Salt and pepper

PREPARATION

- Cut the vegetables into large pieces.
- Mix the dressing ingredients in a cup.
- Pour the dressing over the vegetables and mix well.
- Garnish with cubes of feta cheese

Maya's salad

MAYA'S SALAD + LIGHT BREAD + PROTEIN = PERFECTLY BALANCED MEAL

INGREDIENTS

- 3 cups vegetables (you may use a pre-washed bag of lettuce, carrots, cabbage, and arugula)
- 4 mushrooms, sliced
- 5 walnut halves, unroasted
- 10 cherry tomatoes

DRESSING

- 1 tablespoon olive oil
- 1 tablespoon lemon juice
- 2 tablespoons soy sauce
- 1 crushed garlic cloves
- 2 fresh basil leaves sliced into thin ribbons
- Dash of coarsely ground pepper

PREPARATION

- Mix the dressing ingredients in a cup.
- Pour the dressing over the salad.
- Mix well and add walnuts.

Kosloff cauliflower salad

| TWO SERVINGS

INGREDIENTS

- 1 medium-sized cauliflower
- 2 stalks of celery
- ½ small red onion
- 4 tablespoons chopped walnuts, unroasted
- 2 tablespoons dried cranberries

DRESSING

- 1 tablespoon soy sauce
- 2 tablespoons balsamic vinegar
- 2 tablespoons water
- 1 tablespoon date honey
- 1/3 teaspoon salt and dash of black pepper

PREPARATION

- Thinly slice the outer cauliflower florets with a knife, turning the cauliflower until it is "shaved" on all sides and bits of cauliflower fall into a bowl. Use the remaining cauliflower core for soup.
- Chop the celery into small pieces and mince the red onion. Add both to the cauliflower bits.
- Mix the dressing ingredients in a cup and pour over the vegetables Mix well.
- Add dried cranberries and walnuts.

Honey mustard salmon

| ONE SERVING

INGREDIENTS

- 7 ounces (200g) of salmon or chicken breast
- 1 teaspoon honey
- 1 teaspoon soy sauce
- 1 teaspoon mustard

PREPARATION

- Defrost the fish or chicken in the refrigerator.
- In a deep dish, mix the dressing ingredients.
- Marinate the fish or chicken for 20 minutes.
- While it's marinating, heat the oven to 350°F (180°C).
- Remove the fish or chicken from the marinade and place it on a baking pan lined with baking paper. Bake uncovered for 20 minutes.

Oven-roasted green beans

| TWO SERVINGS

INGREDIENTS

- 14 ounces (400g) French green beans
- 1 tablespoon olive oil
- Thyme and rosemary
- Salt and pepper to taste
- 5 garlic cloves, unpeeled

PREPARATION

- Spread a bag of frozen green beans on a baking pan lined with baking paper.
- Sprinkle a tablespoon of olive oil, spices, and garlic on top of the green beans.
- Gently mix the green beans to allow the oil and spices to spread evenly.
- Roast for 20 minutes in the oven, pre-heated to 350°F (180°C).

Pepper delicacy

| TWO SERVINGS

INGREDIENTS

- 4 bell peppers, cut in strips (use an assortment of colors)
- 1 tablespoon olive oil
- 1 crushed garlic clove
- Salt and pepper to taste

PREPARATION

- Heat oil in a large skillet and sauté peppers over high heat until they begin to blacken.
- Add garlic and spices. Cover and steam for another 15 minutes on low heat, or until the peppers soften.

Radish, corn, and walnut salad

THIS LUNCH IS SO FILLING THAT YOU WILL FORGET FOOD EXISTS FOR FOUR HOURS

INGREDIENTS

- 3 cups of cut lettuce plus 1 cup baby greens
- 5 fresh mushrooms
- 2 radishes, diced
- 10 cherry tomatoes
- ¼ cup corn kernels
- 3 ounces (80g) feta cheese, cubed
- 8 walnut halves, unroasted

DRESSING

- 1 tablespoon olive oil
- 1 crushed garlic clove
- 1 teaspoon mustard
- 1 teaspoon balsamic vinegar
- 1 teaspoon sugar
- 1 tablespoon water
- Salt and pepper to taste

PREPARATION

Mix the dressing ingredients in a cup and pour over the salad.

Frequently Asked Questions

WHAT CAN I USE TO SUBSTITUTE A TABLESPOON OF OIL?

One tablespoon of oil per day is necessary because oil is essential for digestion and absorption of calcium and some vitamins from food. The best oil to use is olive oil, but you may also use canola oil, sunflower oil, or sesame oil. It is also possible to substitute 1 tablespoon of oil with half a medium-sized avocado, 1 tablespoon tahini, 1 tablespoon mayonnaise, 10 olives, or 12 almonds. This tablespoon of oil is not for frying. It should be added to salad or steamed vegetables (after cooking). This tablespoon of oil is a daily requirement in addition to any oil that is called for in our recipes.

WHICH VEGETABLES CAN BE EATEN UNLIMITED?

Almost all vegetables are "free vegetables" and can be eaten unlimited. If you have a meal that includes tomato and cucumber, it is only a serving suggestion. You can replace the tomato and cucumber with any other vegetable. Free vegetables include artichokes, arugula, asparagus, baby greens, bean sprouts, bell peppers, broccoli, Brussels sprouts, cabbage, carrots, celery, cucumber, eggplant, fennel, garlic, kohlrabi, leeks, lettuce, mushrooms, okra, onions, tomatoes, radishes, and zucchini.

The following vegetables are limited to 7 ounces (200g) per day: green beans, pumpkin, and beets.

The following are not considered vegetables: potato, sweet potato, corn, peas, and avocado.

ARE THERE ANY ALTERNATIVE OPTIONS FOR LUNCH OR DINNER?

LUNCH OR DINNER can always be a salad and/or steamed vegetables, with one of the following protein options (weight is after cooking):

OR 7 ounces (200g) of chicken without fat, such as chicken breast, drumsticks, or thighs. Cook or bake the chicken without the skin.

OR 7 ounces (200g) of fish, such as salmon, tuna, trout, mullet, or any other type of fish.

OR 5 ounces (150g) of red meat without fat.

OR 9 ounces (250g) of 5% soft white cheese.

LUNCH can include a salad or cut up vegetables and cherry tomatoes with two sandwiches made with light bread. Each sandwich can be filled with one of the following options:

OR Two slices of cold cuts

OR Half of a hard-boiled egg

OR 1 tablespoon of 5% soft white cheese

OR Thin slice of 9% yellow cheese

OR 1.5 ounce (40g) of tuna fish

OR Quarter of medium-sized avocado

WHAT SHOULD YOU DO IF YOU HAVE A QUESTION AFTER 11 P.M. AND IT'S TOO LATE TO CALL YOUR GROUP LEADER?

Simply go to our website: **www.ykosloff.com/en** On the homepage, you will find a link to frequently asked questions. There you'll find answers about alternatives to cottage cheese, yogurt, and apples, as well as substitutes for light bread, what to do if you want to drink coffee with milk, and many more tips and ideas.

CHECK ✓ IF YOU SUCCEEDED TO:

- ♡ Prepare the recipes
- ♡ Write down everything you ate and how you felt an hour later
- ♡ Eat all five daily meals
- ♡ Walk 30 minutes every day

If you didn't manage to meet at least three of the four goals, try to rejoin one of our groups in the future.

REMEMBER, OUR LEADERS ENJOY YOUR PHONE CALLS. PLEASE CALL US ABOUT ANY PROBLEM, BE IT BIG OR SMALL.

Good luck!

Meeting 2

Private weigh-in

Gift

Present each member with a binder containing menu sheets for Meeting 2.

Getting to know you

The following game is an excellent way for the group to learn names and get to know each other's personalities.

The first person introduces herself with her first name and an adjective that begins with the first letter of her name. For example, Smiley Sarah. If the next

Additions to Meeting 2

TIPS
PAGE 55

EXERCISE
PAGE 60

MENU
PAGE 62

person's name were Abby, she would repeat the first person's name and add her own: Smiley Sarah, Adventurous Abby. Continue around the circle until the last person repeats everyone's names and adjectives.

It's no big deal if you can't remember all the names. Please help out if someone has difficulty remembering your name.

Group rules to encourage weight loss

In my first years of leading weight-loss support groups, some of the groups simply did not work. Being together was enjoyable, but the weight-loss results were mediocre. Sometimes one dominant participant dragged the entire group down. I learned a great deal from these tough experiences, realizing it **is up to the leader to maintain the group rules to encourage weight loss.**

Rule 1

IF YOU DID NOT FOLLOW THE DIET, AVOID SPEAKING ABOUT IT

Anyone who strayed from the diet and ate fattening foods that week should not be permitted to speak about it in the group. We don't want to learn how to overeat. We do want to hear from group members who, for example, attended five parties and still stuck to the diet. How did they manage that?

I ask that anyone who didn't follow the diet to avoid speaking about it with other participants during and outside the group. Talking about overeating brings us down. A participant who finds herself straying from the menu should call me, the sooner the better. After listening to her concerns or struggles, I encourage her to resume healthy eating habits.

2

Rule 2

AVOID DESCRIBING FATTENING FOODS IN GREAT DETAIL TO THE GROUP

It's simply too enticing. In one of my first groups, one of the participants described a new kind of ice cream bar in great detail, announcing that she was able to control herself and avoid eating it.

At the next meeting, it turned out that half of the participants bought this ice cream bar for themselves and did not lose weight. This is how I learned the hard way that weight-loss support groups are not the appropriate setting for talk about fattening foods.

Rule 3

AVOID CRITICISM

The group is not allowed to criticize my comments or those of any other participant. Let me share an example of such criticism. At one meeting, we discussed how to handle eating at social events. Group members offered all kinds of suggestions. I commented that when I attend weddings that begin at a very late hour, I eat dinner before leaving the house. At the wedding, I may eat a salad or a small piece of fish, or maybe nothing at all. This works for me because I ate earlier. Suddenly, one of the participants stood up, evidently very upset, and shouted angrily, "No way, never! That's too much to ask," continuing to explain why she was so angry. After buying a gift, travelling for hours in traffic, etc., how could she not eat at the wedding? As soon as she criticized this idea, I knew she would never even try it. She had also ruined it for others who might have tried my suggestion and discovered that it works perfectly for them, noticing that it is much more enjoyable to dance at a wedding on an empty stomach.

If one of the ideas suggested by me or someone else in the group doesn't suit you or even annoys you, please do not criticize it. Trust me, nobody will be knocking on your door to check whether you've tried it or not. Please, respect every idea – it may be especially useful for someone else.

Rule 4

PRIVATE WEIGH-IN

Give all participants personal space while they weigh in. Some people truly don't want others to know their weight. Keep your distance from the participant stepping onto the scale.

Changing your internal monologue

If you were to wake up in the morning without thinking about anything at all, what's the first thing you would do? ⌛

Let the participants offer answers: go to the bathroom, drink coffee, brush my teeth, etc.

Imagine what it would be like if you didn't have any thoughts. Essentially you would be a vegetable and wouldn't be able to move at all. Everything you do is motivated by your thoughts. When you wake up in the morning, your brain tells you to sit up, stand up, go to the kitchen, and prepare a cup of coffee. When you reach for something fattening to eat, a thought runs through your mind to justify the action. Everyone has sabotaging sentences that allow them to eat fattening foods. You say these sentences both in your mind and out loud.

Let me give you two personal examples:

I used to say, "I need something sweet with my coffee in the afternoon." I frequently said this to others and to myself, just before cutting myself a piece of cake. In fact, I brainwashed myself with this sentence. After constantly repeating it, I believed that I truly needed something sweet, so I didn't even try to avoid eating cake in the afternoon.

The second sentence, which I used to justify eating fattening food at other times, was "I have no will power."

This is an especially horrible sentence because the attitude spreads to other areas of life as well.

Think about similar sentences you regularly say ⌛

RAISE YOUR HAND IF YOU USE ANY OF THE FOLLOWING SENTENCES TO JUSTIFY EATING

- I'm addicted to chocolate. I need chocolate. I'm addicted to something else.
- I'm addicted to carbohydrates. I'm addicted to bread.
- I have self-destructive tendencies.
- I'm hungry.
- I had a bad day – I deserve it. My life is difficult – I deserve something sweet.
- Only a little bit – just one and then I'll stop.
- It's impossible to watch my weight on the weekend. Or any other sentence including the word "weekend."
- I'll start the diet tomorrow. My diet starts on Monday.
- Food is good for the soul.
- I have low blood sugar, or other medical justifications.

Does anyone have a sentence I haven't yet mentioned? ⌛

People who are trying to lose weight say something to themselves before

reaching for the fattening food. The more we say these sabotaging sentences to ourselves and to others, the more we become convinced that they are true. Just like brainwashing. Naturally, we believe other people's sentences are funny or silly, but our own are serious and seem to genuinely justify eating.

Changing this internal monologue will allow us to control our eating. This is the most important exercise that you will have. Understandably, this exercise may sound silly to you, but it works 100 percent of the time. But the trick won't work if you don't do the exercise, which only takes four minutes a day.

Weekly Exercise

REVERSING SABOTAGING SENTENCES

On the exercise sheets that I will pass out, write three sabotaging sentences you say to justify bad eating habits. Reverse the sentences and write the new ones down as well.

For example:

1. A sentence such as "It's impossible to diet on the weekend" can be reversed to "I can diet on the weekend," or "Dieting on the weekend is enjoyable."

2. A sentence such as "I'm addicted to chocolate" can be reversed to "I'm not addicted to chocolate." Truthfully speaking, chocolate is not a hard drug and nobody is really addicted to it. I assume nobody here ate chocolate this week.

3. A sentence like the one I used to say, "I have no will power" can be reversed to "I have will power". Of course, after telling myself thousands of times "I have no will power", I was absolutely convinced that I truly had no control. Consequently, when I did this exercise and wrote "I have will power", my brain immediately told me "That's not true!" The moment you write down your reversed sentences, they will also seem untrue, and that's okay – believe in the exercise and continue.

Is everyone clear on how to reverse sentences? ⌛

Have the group share ideas for reversing sentences. Always include some wording from the original sentence in the reversed sentence. For example, the reversal of "only one" can be "not even one."

Pass out the exercise sheets and ask the group to write down three sentences and their reversals during the meeting.

The exercise is to repeat each reversed sentence 20 times a day. Say each sentence 10 times in the morning while you're still in bed and 10 times at night before going to sleep.

Demonstrate how easy it is to count each sentence on your fingers up to 10.

Let's close our eyes for one minute and say my sentence, "I have will-power," 10 times.

The leader should close her eyes and participate in the exercise, counting to 10 on her fingers

Repeating the sentences 20 times a day has a powerful influence – everyone who does this exercise sees that it works wonders. But the sentences won't deliver results just because you heard about the exercise here. You must repeat them to yourself all week long.

After doing the exercise for two days and repeating the sentence "I have will power" without really believing it, I found myself in my kitchen, opening up the cookie jar. Reaching for a cookie, I said to myself "I have no will power," and brought the cookie close to my mouth. Suddenly, I heard a clear and powerful voice saying "I have will power." It happened just like that. I put the cookie back, slammed down the lid, and left the kitchen. It worked!

Clarifying menu topics

DRINKING WATER

There's a new cream on the market that does wonders for your skin. Even after you lose weight your skin will look tighter and refreshed. Bear in mind that this cream costs $200 and must be applied five times a day.

Will you buy it? ⌛

This cream does not really exist, but there is a way to keep your skin looking beautiful even while you lose weight, and the best part is it doesn't cost anything at all – it only takes a little effort.

You may have already guessed the secret. ⌛

Drinking water makes your skin look beautiful. Fifty and sixty-year-old women who lost weight in my groups had skin that looked younger and more beautiful than ever even after weight loss. The secret is to drink enough. I've been surprised to hear people ask some women who lost weight if they'd had a facelift done. If you generally do not drink a lot and then start to drink 8 cups a day, the difference will be obvious. People may even ask if you got a facelift.

Drinking plenty of water helps you feel full and satiated and encourages normal bowel movements. People who find it difficult to drink should experiment – try drinking water with a slice of lemon, herbal tea, lukewarm water, or cold water. Preparing a nice pitcher of water with lemon slices encourages drinking. I squeeze one lemon into an half gallon (2 liters) pitcher of water and make sure to finish that amount by the end of the day.

NATURAL JUICE

There is only one thing I'm asking you to give up, not only for the duration of the diet but forever: sweet beverages. Even natural juice that you squeeze from fruit or carrots. When you squeeze juice from fruit – for example, two grapefruits – all of the nutritional fibers are lost and only the vitamins and sugar remain. **A lot of sugar.**

How many teaspoons of sugar are there in one small disposable cup of grapefruit juice? ⌛

7 teaspoons of sugar! Drinking a glass of natural juice is like injecting sugar directly into the bloodstream. Blood sugar levels suddenly rise and the concentrated sugar is recognized by the body. In response, large amounts of the hormone called insulin are released which acts to absorb the sugar. Ten minutes later, the blood sugar level decreases, but we remain with high insulin levels and an immense craving for something sweet. As a result, we constantly reach for more and more sugary food. All this happens because of a glass of juice. Is a drink really worth gaining weight for?

SWEET SNACKS

A similar process occurs when we eat sweet snacks. When we reach for a piece of chocolate, we convince ourselves that we'll only eat that one piece. Right from the first bite, however, it's impossible to stop because the body craves more and more sugar.

Beware of another pitfall with chocolate and sweets. Snacking between meals, even eating one date, during the difficult hours before dinner upsets our entire balance. Dinner time finally arrives and we have no interest to eat vegetables. We crave only sweets. If we are careful not to ruin our body's balance by snacking between meals, meal time arrives and we enjoy every bite, saying to ourselves: "Wow, this is more delicious than any gourmet meal, this food truly makes me happy, I should always eat like this!"

If you wish to attain happiness and peace and quiet when eating, remember not to eat even a little something sweet between meals.

MILK

In nutrition, milk is considered a protein food and not a drink. Moreover, milk is very caloric and nutritious. Anyone who adds 1 tablespoon of milk to each cup of coffee will notice that it barely colors the coffee. What does this mean? It shows that she used to add much more milk to her coffee.

Demonstrate the quantity of milk with a small disposable cup.

Look at this small cup. Some people drink 6 cups of coffee every day, half of which is milk. If half a cup of milk contains 80 calories, **how many calories does a person drink in 6 cups? It's hard to believe, but she actually drinks 480 calories per day just from milk.** Even skim milk or milk substitutes are caloric and usually contain 50 calories per half a cup. Try weaning yourself off milk. You are allowed to add a maximum of 4 tablespoons of milk per day.

If you meet a friend for coffee and order a small cappuccino instead of a piece of cake, that's fantastic. Simply count the cappuccino as your 4 p.m. light meal.

TUNA FISH

Tuna in oil is allowed on the diet, but it has to be "washed." Don't be shocked by this proposal. It comes out 10 times better than tuna in water. How do you wash tuna? Open the can partway and slowly pour out the oil until it's all gone. Then fill the can with water and pour that out too. If you don't wash the tuna this way, the amount of oil remaining makes it a fattening food.

Pass out the binders.

SOUP

Please open up to the second page and look at the soup recipe. The vegetable soup listed on the menu is only a suggestion – any vegetable soup will do. Save time on peeling and cutting and simply throw a bag of frozen vegetables into the water. For the majority of people, the soup is very comforting, both emotionally and physically. If you end up feeling that the soup is a life-saver this week, go ahead and prepare vegetable soup every week.

Why is the daily intake of vegetable soup limited to 2 cups (2 ladles)? ⌛

Because we want to shrink the stomach and not expand it with large quantities of soup. It's easy to get carried away with vegetables when they are cooked and soft. If you cook 6 pounds (3 kilos) of vegetables in soup and eat the entire pot in one day, that's a significant amount of calories.

PAYMENT

Please don't forget to pay.

Farewell at the end of the meeting

If one day of the weekly menu doesn't suit you, skip it and do another day twice, or even pick a day from last week's menu.

Don't forget to say the sentences in the morning and at night.

Continue writing down everything you ate during the week and marking the foods you enjoyed. Think about how you felt an hour after eating.

Anyone who follows the menu precisely is guaranteed 100-percent success.

Have a week of good choices.

Tips for Week 2

What to bring to Meeting 2

1 | A gift – a binder for the weekly menus

2 | Week 2 menu filed in each binder

3 | Exercise sheet for each participant

4 | A 200-milliter disposable cup to demonstrate the quantity of milk

5 | Your summary of the meeting's content

6 | Pens or pencils

How to motivate during Week 2

PHONE CALLS

A day after each meeting, I review the cards to see who hasn't lost weight. I call these participants to offer encouragement, asking them what they've eaten since the morning, or since yesterday morning, and what times they ate, listening attentively to their responses.

My goals are:

1. To allow them to speak, which is encouraging in itself.
2. To find one thing to change.

After the participant finishes describing her daily routine, I emphasize that she is already following the diet and doing the majority of the work. Just a little more effort is needed on her part to make another small change.

For example, I say to the participant: "You are at work all day long and you're even taking food along to be able to follow the diet. Essentially you only have to cope with the hours between 5 p.m., when you get home from work and 8 p.m., when you eat dinner. Prepare yourself a glass of water with lemon and a plate of carrot sticks and apple slices when you come home from work. After you finish this light meal, tell yourself, 'Now I am fasting for two hours. I can manage to fast for just two hours – that's easy.'"

Or I may say to the member: "Prepare a recipe for stir-fried vegetables that will last for the next three days and you'll see everything will be easier."

Or: "Write down everything you eat for one week and bring it to me at the next meeting."

If it's obvious from your conversation that the participant is strictly following the diet and is also exercising, tell her that justice will prevail.

It's important to always show confidence in the participant's success and in our weight-loss menu. If you aren't confident, how can she be?

During these conversations, I always focus on just one change. Telling her that she is doing everything wrong will only make her feel discouraged instead of motivating her.

If anyone mentioned difficulties at the weekly meeting, I call and begin the discussion with "I thought about what you said…"

These telephone calls are very important – as a matter of fact, they are the key difference between our groups and other groups. By going above and beyond with your customer service, you really are providing a great service and marketing the diet as best as possible.

Why is it good to be a hesitant leader?

Surprisingly, it is actually helpful to the group when the leader does not have answers to all of their questions, or when she hesitates to answer. Why?

Because this allows someone else in the group to answer. Once another participant responds, she reminds herself what to do in that situation and is convinced more than ever that this is the correct thing to do. Likewise, it is both persuasive and compelling when the whole group thinks together. In other words, don't worry if you don't have all of the answers.

Learn from my experience

WHY ARE THE GIFTS AND PRINTED SHEETS SO IMPORTANT?

People like receiving gifts. Gifts make people happy. Gift-giving radiates generosity on your part because the participants already paid. Moreover, gift-giving makes them want to attend meetings and even motivates them to follow the diet during the week. At the first five meetings, I always bring a gift to hand out. Afterwards, I bring a gift to every third meeting. Make sure that you print the menu sheets and bring them to the meeting. People like to leave the meeting with something in hand. Also, when the sheets are lying in front of them in the kitchen, there is a better chance that they will read the content, buy the products called for in the recipes, and make the recipes. The sheets help participants stay on track.

WHY IS WEIGHING IN IMPORTANT?

Each participant must be weighed in at every meeting. Our participants work hard to keep up the diet and eat correctly in part because they know they will be weighed every week. Being weighed causes us to make changes if we see that we haven't been losing weight. I'm willing to hide the scale and write down the participant's weight without telling her the results until she has lost 20 pounds. Or, alternatively, I allow the member to write down the result on her card without me looking.

FIRST NAMES

The most pleasant sound for anyone is her own name. Devote special attention and effort to calling the participants by their names. When inviting a member to ask a question or share something with the group, say her name. For example, "Yes, Susan?", or "What Susan said now is very important in the weight-loss process. Susan said..." Repeating what someone said gives her the feeling that she was heard and understood, and that the group cares about her. Likewise, repeating a person's first name gives her a good and homey feeling, reminds you and the rest of the group of her name, and creates an intimate atmosphere.

CELL PHONES

If anyone answers her phone, I stop the meeting and we all wait until she finishes the call. This definitely makes her feel uncomfortable, and the other participants learn not to use their phones during the meetings.

TWO COMMENTS ABOUT THE REVERSED SENTENCES EXERCISE:

1. It's a good idea to try this exercise yourself so you'll be able to tell the group about your personal experience.

2. Some people think they don't say any sabotaging sentences, but in fact they do. People say things without understanding that those very sentences enable them to eat fattening foods. For example, "I'm out of control," "I'm going crazy," "I have self-destructive tendencies," "I'm really not interested anymore," or "I decided to cheat on my diet today."

STORIES CAPTURE ATTENTION

Everyone loves a good story. Stories capture attention and listeners will be more likely to remember your message.

The book you are holding is entwined with my personal stories. You have my permission to tell my story as if it happened to you, or you can tell your own.

Don't be afraid to share a personal story, if it's authentic it has the power to bring people closer, especially if your story speaks about your failures. Spontaneously, one by one other group members will be inspired to share personal experiences and an unexpected magic is created in the group.

Story Time

MAINTAINING MY WEIGHT LOSS HAS SIGNIFICANTLY IMPACTED MY LIFE

A month ago, my doorbell rang and outside stood a delivery boy holding a giant bouquet of flowers with a note attached from Melissa. I was moved to tears. Melissa joined my group ten years ago weighing 200 pounds. When she first came, she told me, "I love to eat, but this time I decided to eat right and healthy – to plan my meals and not eat impulsively anymore." Melissa really focused on her goal, revealing seriousness and determination. Within half a year, she lost 40 pounds. In the attached note, Melissa wrote:

Dear Yaffa,

I wanted to thank you because today I am celebrating my 10-year weight-loss anniversary. Of course, from time to time I still struggle, but you gave us tools to cope with those moments too. Maintaining my weight loss over the years has significantly impacted my life at levels deeper than I ever imagined, much more than the number on the scale. For all of this, I want to thank you and wish you continued success teaching women (and some men) that despite everything, it is possible!

Week 2 Exercise

REVERSING SABOTAGING SENTENCES

Let's work on our sabotaging sentences.

Write down three sentences that you say before reaching for something fattening. For example, "I'm addicted to chocolate," "I had a difficult day, I deserve something sweet to eat," "It's impossible to diet on the weekend," or "Just one more and that's it."

1. ____
2. ____
3. ____

Now, reverse your sabotaging sentences and write them down. The reversed sentence probably won't sound right, but write it down anyway.

Some examples of positive sentences are "I'm not addicted to chocolate," "I had a difficult day, so I'm going to treat myself to something that will really make me feel good," "It's possible to diet on the weekend," "Every bit counts," "One is one too many."

MY REVERSED SENTENCES:

1. ____
2. ____
3. ____

Since we've told ourselves these negative sentences thousands of times, we truly believe them. By repeating the reversed sentences, we're undermining those destructive beliefs. Suddenly we're not so sure that eating sweets will make us feel good, or that life is worthless without cake, or that we'll really only take one.

How can we successfully change thoughts that enter our minds intrusively?

BY REPEATING THE REVERSED SENTENCES OVER AND OVER AGAIN.

Repeat the positive sentences at least 20 times a day. Say them 10 times in the morning while you're still in bed with your eyes shut and another 10 times at night before going to sleep.

This exercise produces amazing results! It's especially gratifying to experience the feeling of control in our lives. An extraordinary feeling will wash over you the moment a thought arises that usually gives you an excuse to eat, then the opposite thought will pop into your head, and you'll find yourself leaving the kitchen empty handed.

Week 2 Menu

REPEAT YOUR REVERSED SENTENCES

DAY 1 — sport ✓

BREAKFAST	♡ Beverage: coffee, tea, water ♡ 2 slices of light bread ♡ 2 tablespoons 5% low-fat cheese ♡ Tomato and cucumber slices
10:00 AM	♡ Beverage and yogurt
LUNCH	♡ Beverage: coffee, tea, water ♡ Corn, Radish and Walnut Salad (recipe included in Week 1 menu) ♡ 1 slice of light bread
16:00 PM	♡ Beverage and apple
DINNER	♡ Chinese-style Chicken and Vegetables (recipe included)

DAYS 2, 3, 4 — sport ✓

BREAKFAST	♡ Beverage: coffee, tea, water ♡ Tzatziki (recipe included)
10:00 AM	♡ Beverage and apple
LUNCH	♡ Beverage: coffee, tea, water ♡ Cabbage, carrot, and lettuce salad with 10 unroasted walnut halves ♡ 3.5 ounces (100g) tuna or 1 egg ♡ 1 slice of light bread
16:00 PM	♡ Beverage and apple
DINNER	♡ Beverage: coffee, tea, water ♡ Chinese-style Chicken and Vegetables (recipe included) ♡ Five-color Salad (See website ***www.ykosloff.com/en*** for details)

sport ✓

DAYS 5, 6, 7		
BREAKFAST	♡ Beverage: coffee, tea, water ♡ Omelet made with 1 egg and 1 teaspoon oil ♡ 1 slice of light bread
10:00 AM	♡ Beverage, yogurt, and fresh vegetable sticks
LUNCH	♡ 3.5 ounces (100g) fish or chicken or cottage cheese ♡ Salad made with a variety of vegetables and 10 unroasted walnut halves ♡ 1 slice of light bread
16:00 PM	♡ Beverage and apple
DINNER	♡ 7 ounces (200g) homemade pastrami (recipe included) ♡ Oven-roasted green beans (recipe included in Week 1 menu)

♥ Snack on fresh vegetable sticks and cherry tomatoes between meals ♥ Eat up to 2 cups of vegetable soup per day ♥ Lunch and dinner can be switched ♥ Drink beverages without added milk or sugar ♥ Eat at least 2 cups of vegetables at lunch and again at dinner ♥ One tablespoon of oil per day is mandatory ♥

Recipes

Tzatziki

FOR 10 A.M. OR 4 P.M. MEAL

| ONE SERVING

INGREDIENTS

- 1 yogurt (up to 110 calories per container)
- 2 tablespoons 5% white cheese
- 1 cup cucumbers, cubed
- 2 tablespoons finely chopped dill
- 1 crushed garlic clove
- Salt and pepper

PREPARATION

1. In a bowl, mix together yogurt, cheese, crushed garlic, cucumber cubes, and chopped dill.
2. Add salt and pepper to taste.

We Will Be Fit Soup

| FOUR SERVINGS

INGREDIENTS

- 1 large onion
- 1/3 medium-sized cauliflower
- 1 celery root
- 2 carrots
- 2 zucchini
- Seasoning:
- 2 garlic cloves
- 1 teaspoon salt
- 1 tablespoon olive oil
- Pinch of black pepper
- 2 tablespoons parsley, finely chopped
- Optional: After cooking add a teaspoon of ginger, turmeric or soy sauce

PREPARATION

1 Chop all vegetables into chunks, add 4 cups water, and bring to a boil. Simmer for another 20 minutes and then turn off the fire.

2 Remove half of the vegetables and place them in a bowl. Add chopped parsley to the bowl.

3 Add seasoning to the remaining vegetables in the pot: garlic, salt, pepper, olive oil. Using an immersion blender, puree the vegetables until they reach a creamy consistency.

4 Return the chopped vegetables and parsley to the pot. Taste and add more seasoning if needed.

5 You may need to add ½ cup water to reach the desired consistency.

Chinese-style chicken and vegetables

AN ESPECIALLY SATISFYING MEAL!

| FOUR SERVINGS

INGREDIENTS

- 28 ounces (800g) chicken breast, cut into strips
- 2 tablespoons oil
- 2 tablespoons soy sauce
- 1 small cabbage head, shredded
- 1 scallion, chopped
- Salt, tablespoon of sweet chili sauce, white pepper
- Water as needed

PREPARATION

1. Heat oil in a large saucepan.
2. Add chicken strips and stir-fry on high heat until the chicken turns white. Remove the chicken and place on a plate.
3. Add cabbage, seasoning, soy sauce, and ¼ cup water to saucepan and cook about 20 minutes.
4. Add chopped scallion and chicken and remove from fire.

Homemade Pastrami

MAKE YOUR OWN PASTRAMI - PRESERVATIVE-FREE.

For a wonderful meal eat a pastrami sandwich with 2 slices pastrami and feel satisfied for hours. Another option for a full meal: cut 7 ounces (200g) of pastrami into cubes and add it to a salad.

INGREDIENTS

- 2 pounds (1kg) of turkey breast
- 2 tablespoons of salt
- seasonings to taste for example, mix together 1 teaspoon crushed garlic, 1 tablespoon mustard, 1 tablespoon honey, paprika, and black pepper

Tip: Meat from a female turkey is juicier and more tender.

PREPARATION

1 Dissolve 2 tablespoons of salt in 2 cups of boiling water. Dilute the salt water in four cups (1 liter) of cold water. Marinate the turkey in the salt and water overnight (or for at least two hours).
2 Preheat oven to its highest temperature.
3 Remove the turkey breast from water and pat dry. Rub the turkey with the seasoning paste, making sure to coat all sides.
4 Place the turkey breast, uncovered, on a baking pan lined with aluminum foil. Position in the center of the oven.
5 Bake at the maximum temperature for 20 minutes and then at 320 ° F (160° C) for another 20 minutes.

   IMPORTANT: Turn off the oven and do not open until it cools, at least ½ hour.

6 After the pastrami has cooled completely, cut as thin as possible without the meat falling apart. Keep tightly wrapped in plastic wrap in the fridge for up to 1 week.

Changing our self-perception creates changes in our behavior.

Paul is a taxi driver who weighs 250 pounds. He tells his friends from the taxi company, "I can't lose weight. My whole family is fat and I've been overweight my entire life."

Elaine is a stay-at-home mom who weighs 180 pounds. From time to time, she tries to lose weight, but after just two weeks she gives up and breaks her diet. She tells her friend (over cake and coffee at the café), "Dieting is too difficult – my pantry is stuffed with sweets I have to buy for the children. My kids annoy me because they sit at the computer all day long. My husband annoys me because he doesn't lift a finger at home and when I'm annoyed I binge on chocolate."

Elaine blames everyone but herself - her husband, her kids, and the stuffed pantry. Her failure is brought on by others, and for some reason she doesn't see the hand bringing food to her mouth. Paul, on the other hand, sees himself as a victim of his genetics, over which he has no control.

Paul and Elaine will not change unless they believe that change is possible.

Only when we believe that we can lose weight are we ready to do something about it.

We must avoid self-pity and the tendency to view ourselves as the victim of life's circumstances. The first step in any change is accepting responsibility. If a person doesn't hold herself responsible for her own actions, how can she change?

We must not believe that "people never change" or "a fat person will always be fat" or "I'm destined to be fat." Even a person genetically predisposed to be overweight can learn healthy eating habits.

To create change, we must first change our negative thoughts about ourselves.

PERSONAL STORY

When I was ten years old, I loved reading. I fondly remember going to the public library near my house every day to borrow a book. One day I borrowed a book about a strange boy who performed different types of tests and experiments on himself.

In one of his experiments, he wanted to prove to himself that he had willpower. In order to do this, he decided to fast for a whole day.

This idea intrigued me and I started to fast. It was 2:00 in the afternoon and I had just eaten a big lunch at home. I fasted for an hour and another hour and another hour until I broke my fast at 6:00.

Thinking like a little girl, I reached the conclusion that I had no willpower. From here on, this statement appeared in my life every day, especially when I wanted to eat something fattening. Even as a little girl, I knew I wanted to be thin and that cakes and cookies are fattening. Making excuses for my sweet tooth, I used to say, "I have no willpower."

The years passed and this statement, which I adopted by chance as a little girl, helped me again and again to avoid coping with my tendency to overeat.

Only many years later, at the age of 30, I learned to change my negative internal monologue.

I reversed the statement into a positive one and wrote it down for myself: "I have willpower." Of course, the thought immediately popped into my mind, "But that's not true!" Nevertheless, I continued with the exercise.

Every morning and night, I repeated the following sentence ten times: "I have willpower." Lo and behold my thoughts transformed and subsequently my behavior changed beyond recognition.

What's the moral of this story?

Many times we reach all kinds of conclusions about ourselves by chance at a very young age, while still susceptible. These conclusions accompany us for our entire lives, and not always in a helpful way. For example, a classmate tells a first-grade girl that she's ugly. Unfortunately, she reaches the conclusion that she has to be a good student to compensate for being ugly. Of course, it's not a bad thing that she's a good student, but it's unfortunate that she considers herself ugly at age 20, which is most likely untrue.

Pay attention to negative self-perceptions that reflect something you heard or conclusions you reached during childhood.

HOW CAN WE CHANGE NEGATIVE SELF-PERCEPTIONS?

First, check off the statements you regularly say to yourself to justify reaching for fattening foods, or write down your own original sentence.

"I have to eat something sweet in the afternoon."

"I have no willpower."

"I must have chocolate."

"Life's no fun without chocolate and ice cream."

"It's impossible to diet on the weekend."

"I have to eat to relax."

"I had a rough day, I deserve it..."

"My life is hard, I deserve it..."

"Food speaks to me."

"I'm hungry."

Choose three statements you frequently say to justify eating. Reverse these statements and write them down.

You will be working on these three reversed statements.

Here are some examples:

"I do not have to eat something sweet in the afternoon."

"I have willpower."

"I do not have to eat chocolate."

"Life is fun even without chocolate and ice cream."

"I can stick to the diet on the weekend."

"I can find treats other than food to help me relax."

"I had a rough day, I deserve to enjoy something that is really good for me."

"I deserve to be thin."

"Food does not speak to me."

"I am hungry, so I will eat healthy and satisfying food."

Notice that when you write down the reversed statements, your brain says, "But that's not true." Don't worry, this happens to everyone. Believe in the exercise and continue saying your new statements.

Repeat your 3 reversed statements every day, morning and night, and wonderful things will happen in your life. At the next meeting, share the sentences you are working on and the amazing changes taking place in your life.

Meeting 3

Private weigh-in

Gift

For Meeting 3, I bring every member two disposable pans for baking the quiche.

Getting to know you

Bring a soft 14-inch (35 cm) ball with you to the meeting.

The game is fun and adds lots of laughter to the meeting, as well as creating a great group atmosphere. It's slightly embarrassing to come to a meeting for adults with a toy, but the laughter really works wonders in the group.

Additions to Meeting 3

TIPS
PAGE 84

EXERCISE
PAGE 89

MENU
PAGE 90

Stage 1 | Each participant tosses the ball to someone else and says her own name.

Stage 2 | Each participant tosses the ball saying her own name and the name of the person receiving the ball.

Stage 3 | Each participant tosses the ball saying only the name of the person receiving the ball.

Homework review

Who felt that repeating the positive sentences helped? Is anyone willing to share her sentences with the group? ⌛

Share both your sabotaging sentences and positive sentences with us.

Praise the participants who did their homework during the week and encourage them to share their experiences with the group. Be tough and don't allow participants to speak if they didn't do their homework.

Why are the following sentences especially bad? "My life is horrible, so I deserve something sweet to eat," or "I had a terrible day, so I have to eat something good to compensate." ⌛

Essentially, it pays to take a thick paintbrush dipped in black and paint over our past lives to justify our overeating in the future. However, in this way, we are effectively ruining our lives in the past and our health in the future.

When something terrible happens to me, I immediately think about something sweet. There's no denying it – this is the first thought that comes to mind. Then I say to myself, "the sweet food won't help – it won't solve anything, it will just create more problems." Next I look for a positive distraction. We will speak about creating positive distractions in two weeks.

Another terrible sentence is "Everyone who loses weight just gains it back anyway."

Why is this sentence so terrible? ⌛

Anyone who says this sentence will never succeed in losing weight. If this is a sentence that you repeatedly say to yourself, why should you control yourself and not eat the cake? Half of the participants in my program do not gain their weight back. Therefore, this sentence is factually incorrect.

How many calories in a pound (kg)?

Before embarking on this wonderful process of weight loss, it's beneficial to understand its fundamental principles. Some bodily processes are still unclear – for example, sometimes when we eat sesame seeds or corn, they exit the body undigested in feces. Corn and sesame seeds are very fattening, but if we haven't digested them, are they actually dietetic?

On the other hand, other bodily processes are 100-percent evident but still widely misunderstood by the public. There is good and bad news about these processes. Let's start with the bad news: in order to lose one pound (500g) you need to create a 3500-calorie deficit. This is a solid fact which is impossible to change.

Let me give a few examples to better clarify the topic:

1 The Kosloff Method diet for women is based on 1200 calories. Let's say an elderly woman who cannot exercise does this diet. She exerts 1200 calories of energy per day.

What will happen if she eats according to our 1200-calorie diet? ⌛

She will neither lose nor gain weight.

2 For the next example, let's take someone young who exercises and burns 2500 calories per day.

How many calories does she conserve eating 1500 calories per day? ⌛

On her diet, she conserves 1000 calories per day. In just one week, that is, she conserves 7000 calories, which equals 2 pounds (1kg). In other words, if she follows the diet, she will lose 2 pounds (1kg) a week. This is the group record!

3 For the final example, let's consider the average woman in my groups. She exercises a little, has already passed age 30, and burns 1700 calories per day.

If she eats 1200 calories in a day, she has "saved" 500 calories.

How much will she lose in one week? ⌛

3500 calories – in other words, she will lose one pound (500g) per week.

These cold hard facts tell us that it's impossible to lose 10 pounds (5kg) in one week. Any diet that guarantees quick weight loss is making a promise it can't keep and is significantly detrimental to your health. Of course, some of you have already lost 4 to 6 pounds (2-3kg), but this only happens in the first week or two, when you are essentially losing bodily fluids.

Afterwards, you will likely lose about a pound (500g) per week.

Our goals are to lose weight and to learn how to always eat properly and healthfully while enjoying our food. So it is essential to understand that the weight-loss process is slow and requires lots of patience. Let's imagine someone who is in a rush to lose weight. She chooses the wildest diet in the world: fasting.

If this person exerts 1500 calories of energy per day and fasts for a whole week, how many calories will she "save"? ⌛

10,500 calories, which is only 3 pounds! (1½kg)

Certainly, the scale will show a much greater loss because of the body's loss of fluids during a fast. However, a person who fasts will regain almost everything after a week of eating a balanced diet, except for the real 3 pounds (1½kg). Someone who needs to lose 20 pounds (10kg) cannot fast for seven weeks. Even if this was possible, it would be very unhealthy.

When I was overweight, I read about a puffed rice and milk diet. The diet consisted of eating a bowl of puffed rice cereal and milk three times a day and guaranteed 10 pounds (5kg) of weight loss in five days. I heard about this diet at exactly the right time because I had a wedding coming up in a week and none of my clothes fit. This was absolutely the perfect diet for me, I thought. I don't know if you've ever tried such a severe diet, but puffed rice and milk is the most extreme starvation diet I've ever tried. Looking back, I remember sitting in the kitchen in the afternoon, staring at the box of puffed rice in front of me, and being so hungry I could've eaten the box. But I knew that I had to wait until my "dinner" of puffed rice and milk. In the meantime, I looked at the box and saw that each portion of puffed rice and milk contained 170 calories. I quickly calculated that with that many calories, I could have eaten a big salad with three slices of

light bread three times a day, instead of those famishing puffed rice meals. Suddenly it dawned on me that it's impossible to lose 10 pounds (5kg) in five days. Maybe someone full of bodily fluids could do it. Because puffed rice contains no salt, that diet might cause fluid loss, and temporary weight loss. I knew that I would never be that person, so this crazy diet ended right then and there.

Here comes the good news. We might hear people says things like "I only ate one piece of cake and I gained 4 pounds" (2kg). Nothing in this world comes out of nowhere. Gaining 4 pounds (2kg) from a piece of cake is impossible.

If you eat a big cookie that has 350 calories, how much weight will you gain? ⌛

A tenth of a pound (50g).

Of course, I recommend that you don't eat that cookie. Why? Because it will call all its friends and 10 cookies later, you'll be left with 3500 additional calories and a pound (500g) of additional fat on your body that you don't know how to lose. However, if you skip dessert at the end of a festive meal but taste 1 teaspoon from your spouse's plate, you will still lose weight that week.

Justice will prevail

There is another common difficulty that most dieters experience, which will likely also happen to you during your weight-loss process. The body has the tendency to retain 2 to 4 pounds (1-2kg) of fluids for various reasons: on a hot day, before you get your period, when you're taking medication, after great physical exertion, when you eat salty foods, etc.

If you follow the diet strictly, you likely will be losing a pound (500g) a week. But that week you retain 4 pounds (2kg) of fluids, what will you see on the scale? ⌛

Yes, the scale will show a 3-pound (1½kg) weight gain.

To put it mildly, this can be extremely frustrating after a week of following the menu. Some dieters even contemplate suicide after they see this kind of weight gain. Remember that this happens to everyone during the weight-loss process and justice will prevail. If you follow the diet, in the end you will lose weight, even if it takes another two weeks. Our world is not a fair one. The bad guys kill the good guys. But in the world of dieting, there is justice. If you follow the diet and do not lose weight one week, don't get angry. And certainly don't go home and say, "If I'm not losing weight, I'll just eat whatever I want," because then justice will not prevail. **Let's make a deal: you follow the diet for another week, and I guarantee that justice will prevail.**

Remember – with our diet, justice always wins.

I apologize for translating 1 kilogram as 2 pounds throughout the book. This inaccuracy creates a 10-percent deviation. Numbers have been rounded to make our examples easier to read.

How to make light meals enjoyable

The 10 a.m. and 4 p.m. meals are light, so you should choose food that is both enjoyable and "the final word."

Why are these foods the final word? ⌛

These foods satiate you for at least an hour and a half. Moreover, after eating them you won't think about food anymore. Does fruit satiate you, or does it just whet your appetite? Maybe yogurt is more satiating?

Try to eat plain yogurt, which is real yogurt, rather than substitutes. All of the dietetic yogurts with fruit contain a lot of stabilizers and are unhealthy. In fact, their fruit is really only jam.

I've found that the most satiating meal for me is a sandwich with light bread and a tablespoon of cottage cheese topped with lettuce. This goes well with a cup of coffee. With the calories of the 10 a.m. or 4 p.m. meal, you can also eat corn on the cob, a hard-boiled egg, or 12 unroasted almonds.

If you're the type of person who is always hungry, there is a solution. Meals can be made more satiating by adding vegetables. For example, cut up some carrot and celery sticks, add some thin apple slices, and arrange them on a nice plate. Make tzatziki from the yogurt, adding cucumbers, dill, and crushed garlic.

Another option is to cut a tomato in half, remove the pulp, and refill it with a hard-boiled egg mashed with the pulp, adding a little salt and pepper.

When the time comes for the 10 a.m. or 4 p.m. meal, you don't necessarily have to follow the menu. Just choose from the ideas mentioned above. The most important thing is to feel satiated and happy afterwards. If you've already had a sandwich for breakfast and two sandwiches for lunch, avoid choosing another sandwich for the 10 a.m. or 4 p.m. meal. That's too much bread for one day. Do not eat more than six slices of light bread per day. On the other hand, if you ate protein and vegetables for lunch, a sandwich for the 4 p.m. meal is perfect.

If the morning is easy and you find the evening more difficult, you can have carrot sticks at 10 a.m. and eat the 10 a.m. light meal at night.

Carbs with carbs

Many questions emerge in discussions of the 4 p.m. light meal. For example, can we eat a granola bar or a slice of light bread with a little honey substituted from the salad dressing instead of the 4 p.m. meal?

I stop the meeting and put my lecture on hold, saying that this is a key question and that it's important for everyone to listen and understand.

A granola bar is actually a cookie cleverly packaged to seem healthy, but it is still a cookie. When we eat a granola bar, our blood sugar level rises instantaneously, releasing a large amount of the hormone insulin intended for the absorption of sugar. At the end of this process, we are left with surplus insulin and a craving for carbohydrates.

If we add honey to salad dressing, it becomes negligible when mixed with the salad and doesn't boost our blood sugar levels. These are great foods to eat together because we feel satiated. If we spread the same honey (carb) on a slice of light bread (carb), we are actually preparing a cookie for ourselves, which triggers the very same insulin process that I described with respect to the granola bar.

The concept of carbs with carbs is an important concept, so ensure that the

participants understand it.

Additional examples of carbs with carbs:

1 Imagine taking a recipe for phyllo dough (carb) filled with spinach (vegetable) and cheese (protein), and substituting the spinach and cheese with an apple filling. The combination of phyllo sheets and baked apple is carbs with carbs, so we would essentially be baking ourselves a cake. The body would react accordingly.

2 Light bread with sugar-free dietetic jam. The jam is made from fruit, so it doesn't make a difference that it's sugar-free because it's full of the fruit's sugar.

   A slice of light bread (carb), with cheese (protein), and a tomato (vegetable) is a winning combination that we should eat.

3 Any type of cereal is a pure carbohydrate and can raise your blood sugar (even if it's full of fiber like bran flakes).

Weekly Exercise

HOW TO FOLLOW THE DIET AT SOCIAL EVENTS

Hand out the exercise sheet and pencils.

Social events can be challenging when you're trying to lose weight, so it's wise to find coping methods that work for you. When you anticipate the difficulty, decide how to work through it, and write down your coping method in ink, there is a better chance that you will implement your plan. First, let's complete the table I handed out. Then we'll brainstorm together, and everyone will contribute an idea about how to stick to the diet at social events.

Consider all the events coming up in the next two weeks, whether they're going out to eat at a restaurant, a weekend meal with family, a holiday meal with friends, or a staff meeting where refreshments will be served. Stopping by to see a neighbor who always offers cake is also considered a social event. Be sure to fill in all of the lines in the table you received.

Who has a social event this week and would be willing to share a plan with the group? ⌛

Helpful tricks:

Plan ahead Write down what you will eat at the event. It's a good idea to share what you plan to eat with your spouse or a friend.

Eat beforehand Before leaving the house, eat a light meal like a bowl of vegetable soup or an apple. Arriving less hungry makes it easier to wait for the main course. Enjoy the main course with vegetables on the side.

Bring food along Many times you can bring your own food, like when you visit parents or good friends. Or bring a big salad to share with everyone.

Give advance notice If you wait until the last minute to tell your hosts that you're on a diet, they may try to convince you to eat the food they've already prepared. However, if you tell them a few days in advance that you'll mainly eat salad and ask for their help, they will definitely take the time to prepare it, and you'll be too embarrassed to eat dessert.

Announce to all Sometimes when I'm a guest and there are nuts on the table, I start to wonder whether I should take some or not, and instead of listening to the conversation, I find myself talking with the bowl of nuts. Here, I

use a trick that works wonders: I announce my plan to everyone. I lean forward, push the nuts to the other side of the table, and say "Take these nuts away from me – I don't want to gain weight." Afterwards, I don't think about the nuts anymore and this inner conversation quiets down.

Decide that cake makes you nauseous On my way to meet friends for coffee, I imagine that all cake is disgusting. It's too oily and makes me nauseous. In my imagination, I see myself avoiding the cakes, only drinking coffee or tea, and feeling great.

Only get up once At a party or hotel, only go to the buffet table once. Fill up a big plate with lots of vegetables and some protein and don't get up again.

Daphna's trick Portions are really large at restaurants, but it's hard to eat only half a plate. Personally, I never managed to eat a half portion until Daphna taught me the following trick. I know from experience that it works! After eating half of your food, lean back, put your hands on your stomach, and say "I'm stuffed," just like the skinny people do. Then wipe your mouth with a napkin and place it in the middle of your plate.

Avoid skipping meals

Never skip meals to save calories for an event.

Why is it a bad idea to skip lunch so you can eat more at night? 

Because you'll arrive starving and wind up eating 7000 calories.

Saving costs us dearly.

On our diet, there is also no compensating. Compensation never works! If you overate a little, so what? Get back eating your feel-good foods immediately and don't skip even one calorie. Get back on track without trying to compensate, without making a big deal of it, and without saying a silly sentence like "There goes my diet."

Clarifying menu topics

TWO-PART DINNER

If you get home from work exhausted and starving, a light meal will probably be insufficient. Splitting dinner into two parts is a good option in this case. Eat half of your dinner when you get home and the second half at dinner time. You can look forward to eating your afternoon light meal at 9 p.m.

In general, every meal can be split into two. If you have two sandwiches for lunch, eat one at 1 p.m. and the other at 3 p.m.

Hand out the weekly menu

Farewell at the end of the meeting

Please continue to write down everything you eat this week. When the participants are all getting up and saying goodbye, I call after them: "Keep just this week."

Week 3 Tips

What to bring to Meeting 3

1 | A gift - two disposable baking pans for each participant

2 | Exercise sheet for each participant

3 | Week 3 menu for each participant

4 | Your summary of the meeting's content

5 | Pens or pencils

How to motivate during Week 3

A day after each meeting, I call everyone who missed it and tell them that we missed them. I ask them how it's going and encourage them to come to the next meeting. After someone misses three meetings in a row, I call one last time and then stop calling.

After this third meeting, I call every participant who needs to lose more than 33 pounds (15 kg) but hasn't even lost 4 pounds (2 kilos) yet. When calling a participant who has only lost a few pounds, don't tell her that you think she hasn't lost enough. Tell her you are calling to offer encouragement. Ask her about her eating and exercise habits.

Often you reach the conclusion that she needs to exercise an additional 15 minutes a day. Maybe she is not following the diet precisely enough. Or maybe she is following the diet during the week, but not on weekends. Ask her when she started the diet. It's possible that she is following the diet well and losing weight slowly but surely. If she started the diet two weeks before the group began, you won't see the big loss of fluid that occurs during the first and second weeks of the diet.

Keep your audience awake

MOVE AROUND WHILE LECTURING

While giving your meeting lecture, move around a lot and emphasize each topic with gestures. For example, when speaking about dipping a thick paintbrush in black and painting over your life to justify overeating, mime dipping a paintbrush and turn around to paint an imaginary wall behind your back.

Extra Topics

TRAVELLING ABROAD AND VACATIONING AT HOTELS

This is a topic which can be introduced earlier or later, depending on the questions that come up in the group. Ask participants why it's actually easy to follow the diet while you're staying in a hotel or travelling abroad.

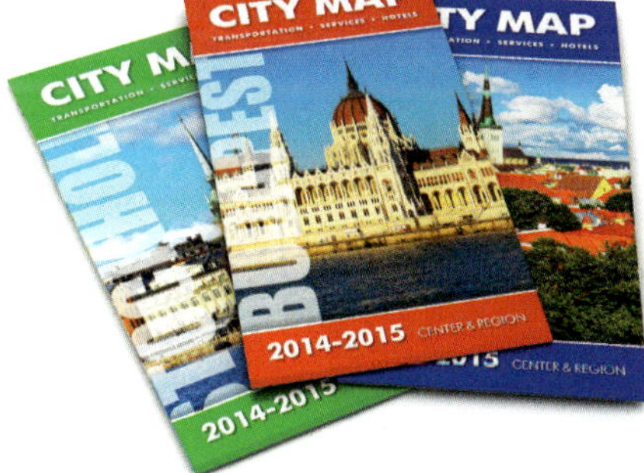

After they've shared some ideas, add your own from the following list:

- Walking a lot helps burn calories.
- Food is not constantly within our reach.
- Focus on the fun things to be enjoyed abroad or on vacation, and not on the fattening foods there.
- It's possible to eat just like you do at home while staying at a hotel.
- Come down to breakfast with your own bread or with a tomato.
- Never skip lunch. It's best to stop and eat a Greek salad on the go. In fact, the Greek salad has become a favorite menu item around the world.

- The worst thing to do is eat a big breakfast and then a big dinner. If you eat this way, breakfast is 1500 calories and dinner is 2000 calories, so you ultimately gain 10 ounces (300 g) per day.
- If you want to taste an interesting new cuisine, choose just one food from all the options and eat it once, on the last day of the vacation.

NOBODY LOSES WEIGHT EATING SWEETS

Isn't it interesting that people who eat something really small but really sweet instead of the 4 p.m. meal don't lose weight? Even if it's just one sweet, and even if it's only a date or a piece of chocolate!

Why does this happen? Why does sweet food stop the weight-loss process? ⌛

In the 30 years that I've been involved in weight loss, I've learned one very important thing: nobody loses weight eating sweets.

There are people who eat just 900 calories a day and should be losing weight beautifully. But their weight stays the same. I interrogate them, asking them to write down every last thing they put in their mouths. It always turns out that they have been eating sweets, usually instead of the 4 p.m. meal. At all costs, avoid eating bread with dietetic jam, or a granola bar, or cereal instead of a meal. Anyone who makes these substitutions will not lose weight.

📖 Story Time

HER FAVORITE HOBBY IS BAKING COOKIES.

I will never forget Nora, a beautiful, tall woman who participated in one of my groups many years ago. 100 pounds (45 kg) overweight, Nora was determined to succeed. She followed the menu precisely and exercised daily. Every week, she lost weight at a wonderful pace. After six months she lost 50 pounds (22 kg), and a year later she was down 80 pounds (36 kg). I vividly recall how weight loss added to her beauty and how her gorgeous eyes would shine. I will never forget one of the stories Nora shared with the group. She was a single mother of two teenage girls. Her daughters never invited friends over to the house, even though she encouraged them to do so. Only after she lost weight did they suddenly start to invite friends over. It took her time to realize that her daughters were deeply embarrassed of how she looked.

Nora celebrated her new look. Her newly developed self-esteem empowered her to exercise and go out walking. When we said goodbye at the end of the year, I was confident that she would maintain her weight loss and even continue to lose the few pounds that remained to her goal weight.

Three years later, one of Nora's co-workers joined my group. She told me that Nora gained all of her weight back and might have even added some more. I was beside myself with shock. My stomach literally hurt all day. I couldn't stop thinking about Nora all week long. Finally I gathered the courage to give her a call. Without wasting a minute, I told her that I heard she regained her weight and asked if there was anything I could have done to prevent that from happening. Maybe I should have convinced her to get weighed-in every other week?

Nora was honest with me and told me she didn't think I could have done anything to help. She shared some information with me about how she regained the weight. Her favorite hobby is baking cookies and she enjoys collecting interesting recipes from all over the world. Over the years, she has gathered many special recipes from her mother and grandmother, including her favorite butter cookie recipe, which was passed on from her great-great-grandmother.

While participating in my weight-loss group, she continued to bake but didn't touch a single cookie. As soon as she stopped coming to the group meetings, she started to eat from her homemade cookies. First one cookie, then only two, until she ended up eating a whole tray of cookies, just like before the diet.

To the leader: *If the topic of hobbies arises at one of the meetings and you hear that one of the members bakes bread, cakes or granola, encourage her to choose a new healthier hobby, such as dancing, ceramics, or painting. If someone has the tendency to gain weight, dedicating her time and creativity to fattening food will not work when it comes to maintaining weight loss.*

Week 3 Exercise

HOW TO FOLLOW THE DIET AT SOCIAL EVENTS

	Event description	How will I eat healthy at this event?
1		
2		
3		
4		
5		
6		
7		
8		

When you write down your decision and share it with others, you're more likely to follow through with it.

Week 3 Menu

CALORIES & WEIGHT LOSS.

HOW TO EAT HEALTHY AT SOCIAL EVENTS

DAY 1

sport ✓

BREAKFAST	♡ Beverage: coffee, tea, water ♡ 2 slices of light bread ♡ 2 tablespoons 2% low-fat cottage cheese ♡ Tomato and cucumber slices
10:00 AM	♡ Beverage and apple
LUNCH	♡ Beverage: coffee, tea, water ♡ 1 slice of light bread ♡ Carmel's Salad (recipe included)
16:00 PM	♡ Beverage and apple
DINNER	♡ Sicilian Layered Vegetables (recipe included) ♡ 3.5 ounces (100g) fish or chicken

DAYS 2, 3, 4

sport ✓

BREAKFAST	♡ Beverage: coffee, tea, water ♡ 2 slices of light bread ♡ 2 tablespoons avocado ♡ Tomato and cucumber slices
10:00 AM	♡ Beverage and yogurt
LUNCH	♡ Beverage: coffee, tea, water ♡ Shakshuka (recipe included) ♡ 1 slice of light bread
16:00 PM	♡ Beverage and apple
DINNER	♡ Beverage: coffee, tea, water ♡ Zucchini Delicacy (recipe included) ♡ 5 ounces (150g) fish or chicken

sport

DAYS 5, 6, 7

BREAKFAST	♡ Beverage: coffee, tea, water ♡ 2 slices of light bread ♡ 2 tablespoons 2% low-fat cottage cheese ♡ Tomato and cucumber slices
10:00 AM	♡ Beverage ♡ Fresh vegetables ♡ 12 unroasted almonds
LUNCH	♡ Beverage: coffee, tea, water ♡ Vegetable quiche (recipe included) ♡ 1 slice of light bread
16:00 PM	♡ Beverage and apple
DINNER	♡ Beverage: coffee, tea, water ♡ Vegetable & Lentil soup (recipe included) ♡ 2 slices of light bread or 3 ounces (80g) chicken

♥ Snack on fresh vegetable sticks and cherry tomatoes between meals ♥ Eat up to 2 cups of vegetable soup per day ♥ Lunch and dinner can be switched ♥ Drink beverages without added milk or sugar ♥ Eat at least 2 cups of vegetables at lunch and again at dinner ♥ One tablespoon of oil per day is mandatory ♥

Recipes

Carmel's Salad

THIS SALAD IS THE HIGHLIGHT OF MY FRIDAY NIGHT MEAL.

I fill my plate with salad and add a small portion of two other dishes served.

INGREDIENTS

- ½ head of cabbage
- 15 walnut halves or pecan halves

DRESSING

- 2 tablespoons soy sauce
- 1 tablespoon sunflower oil
- 1 teaspoon sugar
- ¼ teaspoon salt

PREPARATION

1. Shred the cabbage. Mix the dressing ingredients well and pour over the salad.
2. Using your hands, massage the cabbage in a bowl for about three minutes.
3. Top with nuts.

Sicilian Layered Vegetables

EAT ONE-QUARTER OF THE RECIPE AND USE THE REST TO PREPARE SHAKSUKA

| FOUR SERVINGS

INGREDIENTS

- 2 onions, chopped into large pieces
- 1 eggplant, sliced into ¾ inch rounds
- 1 medium sweet potato about 1/2 pound (300g), peeled and sliced into ¾ inch rounds
- 2-3 zucchini, sliced lengthwise
- 2 tomatoes, sliced into ½ inch rounds
- 4 celery stalks, diced

SAUCE

- 2 tablespoons tomato paste
- ½ cup water
- 1 tablespoon oil
- 1 teaspoon salt
- Juice of ½ lemon
- 2 garlic cloves, crushed

PREPARATION

1. Layer the vegetables in a pot in the following order: onion, eggplant, sweet potato, zucchini, tomato, and celery.
2. Mix the sauce ingredients well and pour over the vegetables.
3. Bring to a boil and simmer for half an hour on low heat.

Shakshuka

ONE SERVING

INGREDIENTS

- 1 portion of Sicilian Layered Vegetables
- 1 egg

PREPARATION

1. Place ¼ of the layered vegetables in a skillet.
2. Make a small well in the middle and place an egg inside.
3. After bringing to a boil, cover and cook for another five minutes on low heat.

Zucchini Delicacy

THREE SERVINGS

INGREDIENTS

- 1 tablespoon oil
- 1 onion, coarsely chopped
- 3 medium zucchini, grated
- 1 egg
- Salt and pepper to taste

PREPARATION

1. Sautee onion in oil in a skillet.
2. When the onion begins to brown, add zucchini.
3. After cooking for seven minutes, add one egg and continue to stir until cooked thoroughly.
4. For vegans: Substitute 5 ounces (150g) of grated tofu for the egg and cook for another five minutes.

Serving options: Eat the entire amount prepared with 1 slice of light bread as a meal or add 5 ounces (150g) of fish or chicken to a third of the recipe.

Vegetable Pie

SERVE COLD OR WARM

THREE SERVINGS

INGREDIENTS

- 2 pounds (800 g) of frozen broccoli or cauliflower (or a mixture)
- 16-ounce (500g) container of 2% low-fat cottage cheese
- 3 ounces (80g) of 5% feta cheese
- 3 eggs
- Salt and pepper to taste

PREPARATION

1 Bring a pot of salted water to a boil. Add broccoli or cauliflower and cook for three minutes. Drain thoroughly.

2 Chop the larger pieces of vegetables into smaller pieces.

3 Return to the pot and add the remaining ingredients. Mix well.

4 Place in a 10-inch (26cm) round quiche pan. (Greasing the pan is not necessary.)

5 Preheat oven to 375°F (190°C) and position the quiche in the center of the oven.

6 Bake for an hour until it browns on top. Using a toothpick, check that the quiche is baked thoroughly. You may need to bake for another 10 minutes.

Vegetable & Lentil Soup

| FIVE SERVINGS

INGREDIENTS

- 1 cup of red lentils
- 2 large onions
- 3 carrots
- 1 cup corn kernels
- 1 tablespoon olive oil
- 1 teaspoon salt
- ½ teaspoon sweet paprika
- **Optional**: add parsley, garlic, black pepper, turmeric or ginger

PREPARATION

1. Boil 5 cups of water in a large pot. Chop all vegetables into chunks and add to the water. Add lentils and corn kernels.
2. Cook for an additional 25 minutes.
3. After cooking, add olive oil and spices.
4. For a creamy texture, puree the soup with an immersion blender.
5. If the soup is too thick, add an additional cup of boiling water to reach the desired consistency.

How to calm your sweet cravings

Drink a cup of hot tea with a half teaspoon of sugar. Enjoy different flavors of tea and drink it either hot or cold. Wait 15 minutes and you'll see that your cravings will be satisfied. Guaranteed!

Options for the 10 a.m. and 4 p.m. meals

Apple and carrot sticks

Hard-boiled egg and tomato

Yogurt (up to 100 calories) and a cucumber

Carrot sticks and 12 unroasted almonds

Make sure to eat the almonds with cut-up veggies and keep the remaining almonds out of reach. If 12 almonds are not satisfying enough, then this light meal is not for you.

The road to success is paved with failures

When we're learning to do something difficult, there will always be failures to overcome.

It's impossible to learn how to ride a bicycle without falling – without practicing and failing a little along the way. Imagine if you gave up after the first or second time you fell off a bicycle and said, "I can't ride a bike. I don't have the talent for it the way everyone else does."

You wouldn't ever know how to ride a bike!

If you quit the first time you swallowed water while learning to swim, you wouldn't know how to swim.

If you despaired the first or second time you burned dinner or botched the recipe, you wouldn't know how to prepare a wonderful dinner for 12 people.

I have a friend who failed her driving test twice and quit her lessons. It's been 30 years and she still doesn't have a driver's license, which can be extremely inconvenient at times. On the other hand, I have another friend who failed the written test three times and the driving test seven times until she finally passed. She's been driving for the past 25 years and has long forgotten the difficulties she had along the way.

Think of something you do well, either at work or at home, and think of the setbacks you had as you learned how to do it. Obviously, if you had given up after the first failure, you wouldn't have learned what you know today.

Close your eyes and think about it for two minutes.

No, DO NOT keep reading – this is important!

Think of something you do well, and connect to the satisfaction you feel when you do it.

There is always a friend who says, "How do you do it? I could never do what you do."

THE ANSWER IS THAT DESPITE THE FAILURES, YOU CARRY ON. YOU CONTINUE TO PLAN AND INVEST EFFORT AND SUCCESS FOLLOWS.

However, this friend believes that you have a natural talent and that everything comes easily to you, without the effort and hours of work. In our diet, the same process takes place. Every person who struggles with dieting and says "I can't stick to a diet" imagines that others have a natural talent for weight loss. Everything probably comes easily to them – without self-control or sacrifice and without any planning or failures.

Let's look at a classic case study of a dieting process that you have likely experienced.

You join a weight-loss program with a wonderful, balanced menu and you decide to stick to it until you lose 45 pounds (20 kg). You stick to the diet with determination for the next three weeks, truly enjoying your boundless new energy. You're thrilled with the way you look and your jeans finally fit again. You lost a whole eight pounds (4kg)!

WHY DO WE FAIL?

Three weeks later, after an especially long day at work, during which you didn't put anything into your mouth, you come home to an empty refrigerator.

As you scramble to put something together for dinner, a little voice in your head says, "I haven't eaten all day." So you allow yourself to grab a sweet snack. Next you reach for something savory and then something sweet again. For the rest of the afternoon, you stuff your face with junk food, as negative thoughts run through your mind. "I'll never lose weight; this diet is like an endless war." Immediately after you finish all the junk food in the house, you silently reproach yourself: "Why can't I stick with a diet? Why am I always tempted by junk food? Why can't I control myself? I have absolutely no willpower."

And so you continue to torment and belittle yourself. And the more you belittle yourself, the less capable you feel. Your anxiety levels and fear of failure skyrocket. You feel you can't take any more, this is way too hard, you've taken on too big of a task, and you decide to give up on your diet.

The minute you decide to quit, your level of anxiety decreases and you immediately feel better.

Yes, it's true: there are no more difficulties to deal with. But there's also no chance you will reach your goal.

HOW TO SUCCEED

If you want to successfully lose weight, you have to pick yourself up after failure and continue with the diet. Obviously, there will be failures along the way, like when you forget to pack a lunch for work, or go out with friends for a special birthday dinner, or have an especially difficult day.

In these types of situations, say to yourself, "I have successfully followed the diet for the past three weeks and I only broke it once." Pat yourself on the back and continue following the diet plan at the next meal.

Learn a lesson from failure. How can you prevent this from happening next time? Say to yourself, "Next time I'll be sure to take a lunch break, even if I'm swamped with work."

Feeling like a failure and being anxious are not signs that you should give up. Don't let these feelings win.

Pick up where you left off and continue eating a balanced diet at the very next meal. You'll be the true winner.

HOW TO SUCCESSFULLY GO FROM 180 POUNDS (82kg) TO 148 POUNDS (68kg)

When I go through participants' weight logs and see how people lose weight, I never find anyone who loses weight every single week – EVER! Nobody loses weight every time.

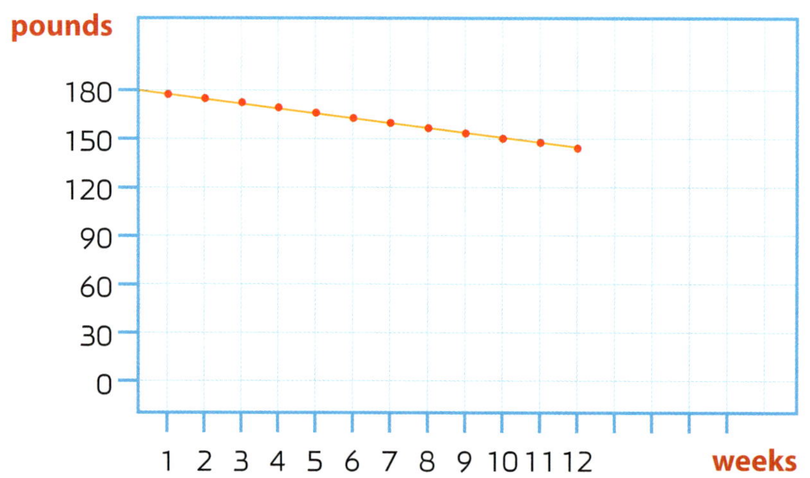

The way a person loses weight looks like this:

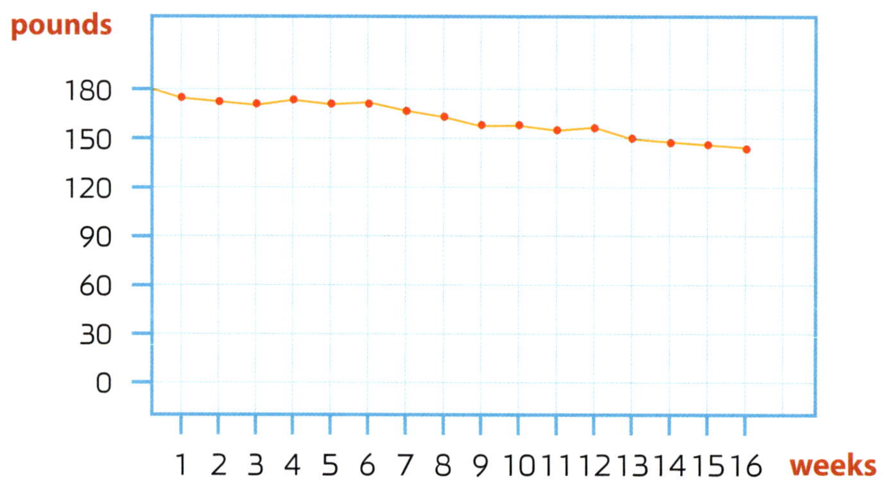

In other words, success is accompanied by weeks when we stumble, and weeks when we follow the diet to a tee and yet the scale stands still.

Losing weight is a process and whoever persists will succeed!

You made a decision to eat a healthy and balanced diet and have gotten on the right track. Now continue and enjoy the way.

Meeting 4

Private weigh-in

Gift

At meeting 4, give a spice plant or pen to every participant.

Getting to know you

Walk around the room and assign every participant the numbers one or two. Move people around so that they will partner with someone they don't know well.

Each person has two minutes to tell her partner three things about herself that she is willing to share with the group, such as her family status, place of work, hobbies, and of course her name. After four minutes, the participants will introduce their partners one by one, in the following manner: "This is David. David is the father of three girls and he likes to paint..."

This game is great because it allows two people in the group to get better acquainted. Also, the participants learn information which wouldn't have necessarily come up otherwise. In one group, there were two young widows who were paired off in the icebreaker game and became instant friends.

Homework review

Who used the event planning chart last week?

(Anne raises her hand). Anne, tell us what you wrote down and what actually happened.

The one method to lose weight once and for all

Is to eat a balanced diet. Let me tell you about my personal experience with the many unsuccessful diets I tried from age 12 to 42. I was always 20 to 30 pounds overweight. I would start a diet and lose about ten pounds in the first month. Then I would eat a piece of cake and say, "there goes the diet," as if I had been granted medical approval: "Mrs. Yaffa Kosloff is permitted to eat as much as she wants." Again, I would start overeating and gaining weight. Shortly afterwards, I would notice that none of my clothes fit and I looked absolutely terrible. Once again, the cycle would begin with a new diet that was soon over.

Saying "there goes the diet" is illogical. I ate a piece of cake – so what? A slice of cake does not excuse you from the diet. I lost ten pounds so nicely and then ruined it with just half a pound. The cake was not a total failure, only a small stumble. Why didn't I continue losing all of my extra weight once and for all? Why didn't I ever reach my goal of looking and feeling terrific? When I stop to think about it, I see how stupid I was to keep holding onto those extra twenty pounds. In any event, I didn't eat to my heart's content and every time I gained another ten pounds, I lost them. This is a phenomenon that happens to all of us. We do not eat whatever we want all the time. Everyone sitting in this room reaches a point at which she tells herself, "Enough, I must put an end to this," and begins to watch her weight.

My only explanation for my illogical behavior in the past is that all of the diets I tried were too extreme.

What is an extreme diet? ⌛

A diet with too few calories and too little food variety.

For example, I tried the "Rabin diet." One day you eat five bread rolls, the next day you eat five yogurts, and the day after that you eat five hard-boiled eggs. Every day you are allowed to eat as many cucumbers as you want. This diet is built on starvation because it has too few calories and lacks vitamins and minerals. The body will not allow you to persist with such a diet for more than two to three weeks. Hunger is the biggest enemy of dieting. A diet in which you are hungry or only eat one type of food will eventually fail, always. When you are very hungry, you also have a need to eat something caloric. You don't crave another cucumber, but rather the most caloric food out there, which contains

both fat and sugar. And once you start eating chocolate, cake, or pizza, you cannot stop.

Our eating plan is balanced. Weight loss is slow and steady, and you will not feel hungry. Persist until you reach your goal weight, even if the process takes a year. After reaching your goal, you can continue with the **same good eating habits**, and even add a few calories, to remain at the same weight forever. The one method to lose weight once and for all is eating a healthy and balanced diet.

How can we successfully avoid the crazy overeating that ruins all of our achievements?

A 250-calorie cookie will ruin weight loss for the day. If we continue following the diet that very same day, we will still lose weight that week. But what does someone like me do, who cannot stop and suddenly finds that she has finished an entire cake? I used to cut a really small slice of cake for myself, and eat it straight out of my hand as I stood by the refrigerator. Sometimes I would buy a box of cookies for the kids and then suddenly all of the cookies were gone. Eating an entire box of cookies is extremely fattening – it adds a few pounds to our weight. And at about the same time the next day, we'll begin searching for something similar to eat. Excessive eating disrupts our entire system. After we binge it becomes difficult to continue eating a balanced diet, and we begin a period of overeating.

This type of binge eating is familiar to most people. Most of you already know the horrible physical and emotional feelings that follow. Disgust, indigestion, and burping up the smell of rotten eggs the next day. It's not like we eat a whole box of cookies and say, "This was the best day of my life."

Absolutely not – the exact opposite is true.

I developed a trick for this type of binge eating. The trick is somewhat difficult, but it works well. Thanks to this trick, I no longer eat entire boxes of cookies, and this makes all the difference between successfully maintaining my weight or not. When we overeat a little, it's possible to continue the diet immediately, on the very same day. Simply continue as usual, without trying to compensate.

My trick works as follows: Let's say a guest arrives from Belgium with delicious cookies, and I place them high up in the pantry. This is the first rule for avoiding sweet snacks. Wrap up the sweets and put them far away so they are not within eye contact and certainly not within hand's reach. The next morning, I am home alone and dying to taste a cookie. At that moment, the internal dialogue that we all are familiar with begins: "only one, it's not so terrible, they are very small, probably only 50 calories per cookie." I grab a chair to climb onto the counter and take out one cookie, putting the rest back. I place the cookie on a plate (I don't eat from my hand standing up anymore), prepare myself a cup of tea, sit down, and slowly eat and enjoy myself.

What happens two minutes later? ⌛

I want another cookie. At this point, I firmly say to myself: "Mrs. Yaffa Kosloff, it's not so terrible if you take another cookie, but if you do, then throw the rest away. Otherwise you'll finish the entire package." Now, this persistence is essential to successfully maintaining our weight loss forever. I know the threat I've made is serious, and sometimes I don't take another one. But other times I can't control myself. Boiling water for tea, I climb back onto the chair to bring down the cookies and place one nicely on my plate. With determination, I throw the rest of the cookies into the garbage, pouring them out of the package and crushing them aggressively so heaven forbid I won't take them out. At last, my prize awaits me - a hot cup of tea and one cookie!

A few hours later, my husband Ronnie comes home and asks, "Where are the cookies from Belgium?" I answer, "I threw them away." Ronnie says sadly, "Why? I wanted to eat one." To which I answer, "Would it be better if none were left because I ate them all?" And Ronnie answers, "No, of course not, good thing you threw them out." Honestly, it is more important for him that I watch my weight. Would it have helped if I were the garbage can? In any case, he wouldn't be left with any cookies to eat.

The rule of thumb is to throw everything away immediately after the guests leave. Yes, I know, someone baked something really delicious for you, and why should you just throw it out? But let's be honest, who is going to eat it? Undoubtedly, it will be either you or someone else in the family who has a tendency to gain weight. Whoever took the trouble to prepare something and bring it over wanted to make you happy, not harm your health. Enjoy the attention and throw it out.

What about the children? ⌛

Why should children, even if they are thin, eat unhealthy food?

A very important commandment in the Bible is "To carefully guard your souls." Throwing out the junk food guarantees that we will take care of our bodies and souls.

Let me share a secret with you: some people hear what they want to hear. In every group, some participants reach the conclusion that I said the Kosloff method allows one cookie a day. That's definitely not what I said. Eating one cookie every day will ruin your weight loss for that day. This one cookie disrupts the entire slow and steady weight-loss process. I know it's hard to believe, but someone who completely refrains from eating sweets is more satiated and has fewer cravings for sweet food. In order to experience this, you must absolutely avoid eating sweets for three weeks. Believe me, it sounds more difficult than it actually is. If you refrain from eating sweets for a few months, I guarantee that your desire for them will lessen. Truthfully speaking, someone who carefully follows the diet will have an easier time than someone who ruins it every day or every weekend. Gradually, the whole weight-loss process becomes much smoother.

Don't skip meetings until you reach your goal

In each group of 20 participants, approximately two people disappear after four or five meetings. To ensure that this does not happen to you, let me first explain how it occurs. A participant sits at home and eats something fattening. Afterwards she says to herself, "This week I won't go to the group. Next week I'll be better."

What does she do from that minute on? ⌛

You got it! She eats an unlimited amount of fattening food. But after she eats so many sweets, it becomes very difficult to continue following the diet. So she fails again the following week, and says again, "Next week I'll be better," and we never see her again. Don't allow this to happen to you. You didn't follow the diet? Okay, it's no big deal. **Nonetheless, it is important to attend the meeting and weigh in, especially after a week when you didn't follow the diet perfectly.** If you can't attend the meeting that week, come to my house to be weighed. When you know without a doubt that you will be weighing in, deviation from the program will lessen and weight gain won't be so terrible.

Physical exercise

Who has started to exercise and is enjoying it? ⌛

Commonly a participant tells the group how much more energy she has had since starting to exercise and how much fun it is to walk, which inspires others to jump on the bandwagon. Often members share ideas about belly dancing classes, or they recommend a fitness center in the neighborhood or a great personal trainer. Review the topic of exercise every three to four meetings because it is important that everyone starts moving.

Studies on people who lost weight and stayed thin found that all of them added daily exercise to their schedule. My perspective is that you will be a happier person if you add daily exercise to your life. You do not need to change your financial status, marital status, or even the political situation – just add exercise to your daily schedule. This is a small effort that brings great rewards.

Eating meals at regular times and the internal clock

Some people are alert during the day and sleepy at night, while others come alive when the sun sets. Similarly, with eating each of us has a different kind of biological clock. If we eat at specific and regular times, the body will become accustomed to this schedule and we will be hungry at exactly those times. If we consistently each lunch at 1:00 p.m., the body will adjust within three weeks. As we start to feel hungry and take a look at the time, incredibly the hour is exactly 1:00 p.m., as if we had swallowed a clock.

What is the advantage of being hungry at regular hours? ⌛

When we get hungry at our regular meal times, chances are good that we will eat one of the diet's planned meals. On the other hand, if we get hungry at odd hours like midnight, we are more likely to eat junk food.

Weekly Exercise

SETTING A REGULAR EATING SCHEDULE

To experience the feeling of calm and serenity that comes with eating at regular times, you first need to set meal times and stick to this schedule for three weeks. On the exercise sheet, write down the hours at which you plan to eat. Try to create a gap of two, three, or four hours between meals.

Over the next two weeks, track your hours by checking off the times when you ate on schedule.

If you don't eat at the scheduled time, write down when you actually ate. Pay attention to the connection between not eating at the scheduled times and breaking the diet.

The 1.5-hour fast after each meal

After each meal, notice the time you finished and do not eat anything else for an hour and a half, not even a carrot. If there are certain hours when you're constantly snacking, say to yourself, "I can manage an hour and a half." Nobody is asking you to fast for a week or even a day, just an hour and a half. Of course, drinking is permitted.

Personally, I'm always still hungry after finishing lunch, and I only feel satiated half an hour, or sometimes even an hour, afterwards. I've learned to simply wait. Continuing to snack doesn't help me feel satiated. The body appreciates these breaks between meals – it has time to calmly digest the food and produce the maximum benefit from the food's vitamins and minerals. Within two days, you'll already feel more energetic. This method of taking breaks between meals also helps us to stop opening the refrigerator every time we are bored or not in the mood for housework. Maybe something has magically appeared there that is both calorie-free and delicious?

Hand out the weekly exercise and pencils.

Clarifying menu topics

SALAD SIZE

Eating large quantities of vegetables is essential to feeling more satiated. Take one bite of protein for every two bites of vegetables. A typical salad should include two tomatoes, two cucumbers, one bell pepper, and half a cup of leafy greens. If you're not in the mood for fresh salad, prepare stir-fried, steamed, or baked vegetables. Make sure you're not neglecting the vegetable portions. A meal that only consists of one piece of chicken and one tomato will undoubtedly leave you hungry an hour later.

To conclude, here is a wonderful saying I picked up from another group leader and friend, Aya Rubinfeld: **A big salad, a small woman.**

REGULAR BREAKFAST ROUTINE

Eating breakfast is extremely important. People who eat breakfast regularly will be less hungry in the evening. The body has been fasting since the night before, and if we skip breakfast it will sense that food is scarce and then reduce its metabolism. Eat breakfast within two hours of waking up. People who wake up at 7 a.m. should eat before 9 a.m. Likewise, people who wake up at 10 a.m. should eat no later than noon. When we eat breakfast, the body gets the message that food is not lacking and our metabolism will speed up.

Some people are satiated from a breakfast of carbohydrates, like bread or fruit, while others feel satisfied for longer if they eat a breakfast of proteins, like cheese, yogurt, or eggs. Notice which group you belong to.

Over the next two weeks, try a variety of breakfast choices from the menu and decide which meals are tastier and more satisfying to you. After you have sampled different breakfast choices for a few weeks, I recommend choosing one routine breakfast to begin your day with, each and every day.

What are the benefits of eating a routine breakfast? ⌛

1 | **No hesitation.** With my eyes closed, I heat up two slices of light bread in the microwave or toaster, add a slice of cheese, tomato, cucumber, or red pepper, and sit down to eat.

2 | The ingredients for my breakfast are always readily available.

3 | **We choose a feel-good meal.** This is the meal that we chose for ourselves, with only ourselves in mind. A meal that sits well in our stomach, in addition to being tasty, calming, and satisfying for at least two to three hours.

While writing this chapter in Santa Barbara, California, I notice people going out to lunch at noon. Perhaps that's because they only ate cereal for breakfast.

EATING OUT AT RESTAURANTS

Be sure to choose restaurants that serve foods and portions suitable for you, such as salads, quiches, vegetable soups, and fish. Naturally, the best choice is salad. Eat slowly, fully enjoying your meal while the others finish their first, second, and third courses. Choose from a variety of salads, including house salad, Caesar salad, farmer's salad, nicoise, and others. The salad may include nuts, cheese, or eggs because this is your meal and you should enjoy it. Ask the waiter not to serve the table rolls (not even for the others) and to serve the dressing on the side.

You may add a tablespoon of dressing to the salad – you are not being punished. Try to minimize the number of times you eat out and find other types of entertainment.

Almost without exception, the food at restaurants is more fattening than at home – the portions are larger and there is more salt.

FRUIT

During the first month, I insist that participants only eat apples and tell them that questions about fruit variety are welcome at Meeting 5. People with a tendency to gain weight get hungry after eating sweets – sometimes even after eating a sweet fruit. Apples are a very satiating fruit. After a month has passed and someone in the group asks about eating a greater variety of fruit, I list other fruit options.

When an apple appears on the menu, you may also eat an orange, half a grapefruit, a large tangerine, half a pomelo, two cups of strawberries, three kiwis, one nectarine, or a small pear. Be cautious and notice if one of the fruits

you started eating again whets your appetite for sweets

There are some fruits that you should not eat: dates, bananas, figs, watermelon, grapes, persimmons, and mangoes. These fruits cause our blood sugar to rise and boost our appetite, so they must be completely avoided for the duration of the weight-loss process.

Hand out the weekly menu.

Farewell at the end of the meeting

I wish you a successful week. Remember, there is no such thing as "there goes the diet" or "the diet is over." This is not a diet – this is a way of life. Even if you overeat, just pick up right where you left off and get back on track.

Week 4 Tips

What to bring to Meeting 4

1 | A gift – pen or another small gift

2 | Exercise sheet for each participant

3 | Week 4 menu for each participant

4 | Summary sheet of the meeting's content

5 | Pens or pencils

How to motivate during Week 4

PERSONAL PHONE CALLS

I am positive that you've already started enjoying the rewarding work of leading weight-loss groups. Occasionally, I'm feeling a little down or sick, but with every last ounce of strength I come to lead my group. Lo and behold, I leave the meeting feeling wonderful both physically and emotionally, almost as if I'm flying on high. However, there is one part of the work that is somewhat uncomfortable – calling participants. But here lies the difference between our groups and others, the personal phone calls between the leader and participant. How do I manage? My policy is to make the calls the day after the meeting and not to call more than seven people at a time. Sitting down with the telephone in the morning, I call those who were missing, those who didn't lose weight, and those who said they were struggling during the meeting. If there's no answer, I leave a message like, "I called to offer encouragement, please call me when you are available," or "We missed you at the last meeting, I'd be happy to hear from you."

If someone answers, I start the conversation with "I called to offer encouragement, is now a good time to talk?" After speaking to seven people (not counting the ones I left messages for), I take a break and call another seven people later in the afternoon or evening.

WHATSAPP GROUP

Before the group's first meeting, create a WhatsApp broadcast list in which the members can only contact you. Send a reminder about the meeting's time and location, a shopping list, and words of encouragement. After the second meeting, make this list an actual WhatsApp group, in which all members can send pictures of their salad or share ideas. Give clear instructions about the group's rules and check to make sure they are implemented. Nobody is permitted to send any unrelated messages (even really funny ones) to the weight-loss group, especially not pictures of fattening food.

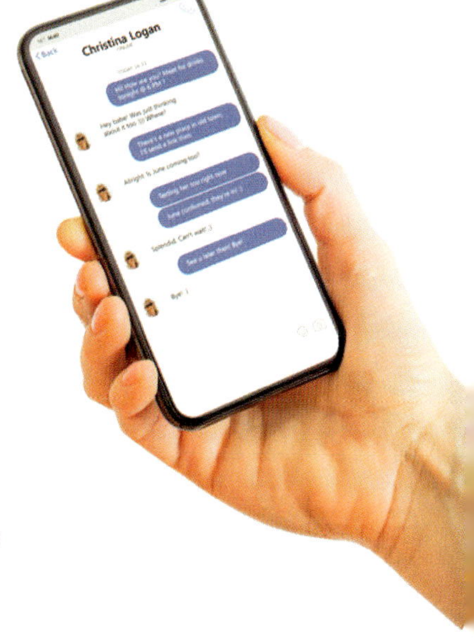

Extra Topics

DIFFICULT SITUATIONS

People have the tendency to overeat under different circumstances. Some people overeat when home alone, while others eat compulsively when they are guests at someone else's home or at a restaurant, and still others eat too much when they are hosting guests. Many of us control ourselves while the guests are there, but as soon as they leave, we eat all the leftovers. A great trick for after the guests leave is to bring the garbage can to the living room and throw out everything, or to ask someone else to put it all in the freezer.

At times we give up the diet altogether because we don't see any results despite all of our hard work. Remember, justice will prevail in the end. Somewhere out there is a notebook with a record of all the weeks we followed the diet, and eventually the weight loss we deserve will show on the scale.

Often when we aren't feeling well, we're under the impression that eating will make us stronger, especially as we near the end of an illness. Try to remember that you will be stronger in a few days and that food doesn't boost your strength.

Pay attention to the fact that appetite comes with eating, and a limited appetite comes with limited eating. Exactly the opposite of what seems logical!

MORE ABOUT THROWING OUT FOOD

There are some people who do not want to throw away food because of the starving people in Africa. If you feel bad about the starving people in Africa, find a way to contribute to people facing hunger.

Some people say it is against their religion to waste food, but it is also against religion to ruin our bodies.

Try this exercise with the group

Let's be silent for a moment. Close your eyes and remember a time when you bought food for the kids or guests and finished it all. Everyone here can remember the times when she opened a package and told herself she would only take one, but then took another and another until entire package was gone and nothing was left for anyone else – not even for the guests she bought it for.

End each meeting with a small summary

What did we learn today? We learned that there is no such thing as "there goes the diet." Also, our homework for this week is to keep track of our eating schedule and try to eat at exactly those times every day.

Learn from my experience

ASK THE GROUP FOR HELP

It may seem inappropriate to ask participants for help. But when someone is able to help, she feels like a partner, and this is excellent for creating a sense of belonging in the group. Next week is the salad workshop, so ask each participant to bring something – disposable bowls, a loaf of bread, plastic forks, etc.

WHAT'S MISSING FROM THIS WEEK'S MENU?

During my first two years of leading weight-loss groups, the Week 4 menu included brown rice mixed with wild rice. Lunch consisted of a cup of cooked rice with a vegetable salad. It took me two years to realize that nobody had lost weight at the fifth meeting. As soon as I removed the rice from the menu, this phenomenon ended.

Why did this happen? There are two possibilities. First, it is possible that some people ate a few extra spoonfuls of rice straight from the pot every day. Second, a meal that consists of rice, even if it is brown rice, dramatically raises blood sugar levels, which causes sugar levels to drop afterwards. When blood sugar levels drop, we feel hungry and begin to search for food.

Celebrate when a participant lose 20 pounds (10kg)

When a member has lost 20 pounds, there is reason to celebrate. The guest of honor tells the group how great she feels after shedding those extra pounds, and she receives a small gift. Personally, I spend about $5 on the gift. It's a good idea to buy the same gift for each member who reaches this goal and attach a nice note.

When the first member of the group loses twenty pounds, I speak with her privately before the celebration. Her attitude toward this short speech will set an example for the whole group. That's the way it is in a group – whatever the first person does, everyone else will do. Ask her to share five things that are fun about her new weight and provide some examples: buying new clothes, climbing stairs without being out of breath, being able to sit cross-legged, skipping her afternoon nap, not snoring anymore, having more energy, feeling less tired in the evening, receiving compliments, etc.

Warn her not to say, "I haven't lost anything yet – I have so much more to lose."

The speech and celebration motivate everyone in the group to reach this goal!

In one of the groups, the first participant to lose twenty pounds amused us all with the story of how her bra got bigger and bigger, slowly climbing up to her neck until it became a bra-turtleneck. She set the standard for humorous speeches. Two weeks later, the next participant shared that she liked to take baths, but before her weight loss, the hot water at the front never mixed with the water at the back – she filled up the whole bath. Now, finally the water mixed easily. A third participant from the same group read a poem aloud at her celebration, proclaiming that as levels of overeating decrease, levels of sex drive increase.

Payment

The customary payment method in my groups and the logic behind it

1 | Attract many participants to Meeting 1

The first meeting is not an introductory session, but you should offer it for free or for a token amount of money. When people know the meeting is free, it is easier to convince them to attend. Occasionally someone tells a friend she is going to a meeting in the evening, the friend comes along, and in the end the friend is the one who actually stays in the group.

2 | Commitment

After the participants try Week 1 of our diet plan, they have to make a decision about joining the group. A participant who wants to attend Meeting 2 must pay for the next six months. Consequently, right at Meeting 2 we have a serious group of people, committed to working hard, and all the participants who did not have the willpower to persevere through the first week have dropped out. This filtering also greatly reduces objections in the group.

3 | Collecting the money

Collect money for six months in advance. Explicitly tell the participants that they are only committing to the first three months, but they have to pay for the entire period. If they decide to drop out after three months, the balance will be refunded to them.

In effect, not demanding payment for all three months sets the participant up for failure because the moment she overeats, she will tell herself, "Good thing I didn't pay for all three months yet," and drop out of the group. **Be assertive when it comes to payment – it actually helps participants stick to their commitment!!** Remember that you are doing them a favor by asking for payment, because if they stick with the diet, they will learn to eat healthily and lose weight. The benefits will be mainly theirs.

Many times, despite the request for a six-month payment, people only pay for three months. Don't wait for them to bring more checks and don't make a big deal about it. Put a colored post-it note on the participant's personal card and write in big bold letters, "OWES THREE CHECKS." Each time the member weighs in, remind her nicely that she still needs to pay. Believe me – she will pay within two to three weeks.

4 | How much to charge

A low monthly price will help you fill up the group at the beginning, even without advertising. When you become better known and sought-after, you can raise the price gradually. I usually charge more for the first three months than for the last, to encourage people to stick with the program for another three month. When fewer people drop out, more participants achieve weight loss of 30 to 40 pounds, and they serve as a great advertisement for the groups. Everyone they meet asks them, "How did you do it?"

5 | Golden advice

Be sure to announce the payment terms at the first meeting because otherwise someone will always say, "You never said…"

Story Time

A PUZZLING PHENOMENON

A month after I started a new group, Lisa called. Lisa had heard about my group from her best friend and insisted that I start a new one immediately because she couldn't wait for the next group I'd scheduled. I responded that I didn't have enough people for a new group, so Lisa promised to bring ten friends to the meeting. I declined politely, but Lisa wouldn't give up. She called every day, telling me that she already had a group of fifteen friends eagerly waiting for the group to start. Eventually I gave in and agreed to start a new group.

Five of Lisa's closest friends attended the meeting, but guess who didn't show up.

I know it's hard to believe, but Lisa didn't come!

Lisa called the next day and promised to attend next time.

Three women attended the second meeting, and Lisa was not among them. Now I was forced to continue leading this small group on an inconvenient day and at an inconvenient location.

All leaders who use the Kosloff Method have experienced this puzzling phenomenon. Some people are willing to trouble themselves to convince the leader and their friends to start a group, but they're not willing to make even a small effort to lose weight. There is a simple solution to this situation: ask the person who claims to represent a group of potential members to give you a list of names and telephone numbers. Call each person to find out if she is really interested in joining the group.

Week 4 Exercise

SETTING A REGULAR EATING SCHEDULE

Treat yourself and your food with respect. Eat feel-good foods at regular times, seated at the table.

Step 1

Record meal times that suit your daily schedule in the table below. Leave a gap of at least two but no more than four hours between meals.

I eat breakfast at:	:
I eat the 10 a.m. light meal at:	:
I eat lunch at:	:
I eat the 4 p.m. light meal at:	:
I eat dinner at:	:

Step 2

Follow your eating schedule throughout the day and check off the meals that you eat on time. If you don't eat a meal on time, write down the time when you actually ate.

	BREAKFAST	10 A.M. LIGHT MEAL	LUNCH	4 P.M. LIGHT MEAL	DINNER
Sunday					
Monday					
Tuesday					
Wednesday					
Thursday					
Friday					
Saturday					

Step 3

At the end of each meal, note the time and do not eat anything for the next hour and a half (beverages are allowed).

You'll be surprised by the wonderful physical feeling that comes with a regular eating schedule. I'm not exaggerating when I say that waiting an hour and a half between meals is a life-changing gift.

Week 4 Menu

SET A REGULAR EATING SCHEDULE FOR YOURSELF.

THERE IS NO SUCH THING AS "THERE GOES THE DIET"

sport ✓

DAY 1

BREAKFAST	♡ Beverage: coffee, tea, water ♡ 2 slices of light bread ♡ 2 tablespoons 2% low-fat cottage cheese ♡ Red pepper
10:00 AM	♡ Beverage: coffee, tea, water ♡ 10 walnuts and vegetable sticks
LUNCH	♡ Beverage: coffee, tea, water ♡ Niçoise Salad (recipe included) ♡ 1 slice of light bread
16:00 PM	♡ Beverage: coffee, tea, water ♡ Apple & Carrot Delight (recipe included)
DINNER	♡ Beverage: coffee, tea, water ♡ Chicken Stir-Fry Salad (recipe included) ♡ 1 slice of light bread

♥ Snack on fresh vegetable sticks and cherry tomatoes between meals ♥ Eat up to 2 cups of vegetable soup per day ♥ Lunch and dinner can be switched ♥ Drink beverages without added milk or sugar ♥ Eat at least 2 cups of vegetables at lunch and again at dinner ♥ One tablespoon of oil per day is mandatory ♥

Hunger is the biggest enemy to eating healthy.

DAYS 2, 3, 4

sport

BREAKFAST	♡ Beverage: coffee, tea, water ♡ 2 slices of light bread ♡ 2 tablespoons avocado ♡ Tomato slices
10:00 AM	♡ Beverage and yogurt
LUNCH	♡ Beverage: coffee, tea, water ♡ 5 pieces of sushi* or 7 ounces (200g) of fish ♡ Large vegetable salad ♡ Vegetable soup *Eat sushi pieces with soup and salad otherwise you won't feel full after the meal.
16:00 PM	♡ Beverage and apple
DINNER	♡ Beverage: coffee, tea, water ♡ Lettuce, cabbage, and carrot salad ♡ Zucchini Quiche (recipe included) ♡ 1 slice of light bread

DAYS 5, 6, 7

sport

BREAKFAST	♡ Beverage: coffee, tea, water ♡ 2 slices of light bread ♡ 2 tablespoons 5% low-fat cottage cheese ♡ Tomato and cucumber slices
10:00 AM	♡ Beverage and apple
LUNCH	♡ Beverage: coffee, tea, water ♡ 5 ounces (150g) Chicken thigh, skinless ♡ Fresh salad ♡ Crispy Vegetables (recipe included)
16:00 PM	♡ Beverage ♡ 2 slices of light bread and 1 tablespoon avocado
DINNER	♡ Beverage: coffee, tea, water ♡ Vegetable & Chickpea Soup (recipe included) ♡ 3.5 ounces (100g) fish or chicken ♡ 1 slice of light bread

Recipes

Niçoise Salad

TWO SERVINGS

INGREDIENTS

- 2 cups romaine hearts
- 2 tomatoes
- 2 cucumbers
- 1 pickle
- 1 small red onion
- 1 hard-boiled egg
- 5.5 ounces (160g) tuna
- 6 olives

DRESSING

- ½ teaspoon Dijon mustard
- 1 tablespoon olive oil
- 1 tablespoon lemon juice
- Salt and pepper to taste

PREPARATION

1. Shred romaine hearts, cut tomatoes into large slices, and cut cucumbers and onions into rounds.
2. Arrange vegetables attractively on a plate.
3. Mix the dressing ingredients well and pour over vegetables.

   Arrange four chunks of tuna and two egg halves around the edge of the plate, and put olives on top of vegetables.

Apple & Carrot Delight

A GREAT SOLUTION FOR ANYONE LOOKING TO EAT SOMETHING SWEET IN THE AFTERNOON

| ONE SERVING

INGREDIENTS

- 3 carrots, grated
- 1 apple, cubed
- Juice of ½ lemon
- ½ teaspoon sugar

PREPARATION

1. Grate carrots and cut apple into cubes.
2. Mix lemon juice and sugar well and pour over the apple and carrot mixture.

Chicken Stir-Fry Salad

THREE SERVINGS

INGREDIENTS

- 1 pound (500g) chicken breast, cut into strips
- ½ head of iceberg lettuce, cut into strips
- 15 cherry tomatoes

MARINADE

- ¼ cup soy sauce
- 3 tablespoons lemon juice
- ¼ cup white wine
- 4 garlic cloves, crushed
- 1 tablespoon olive oil
- ½ teaspoon ground ginger
- ½ teaspoon salt and a pinch of peper

PREPARATION

1. Using a sharp knife, slice the chicken into quarter-inch strips.
2. Marinate the chicken strips and refrigerate for at least one hour or preferably overnight.
3. Remove the chicken strips from the marinade and stir-fry in a hot non-stick skillet without oil for approximately five minutes.
4. Arrange lettuce and tomato on a plate and top with a third of the chicken strips. Refrigerate the remaining chicken for two additional meals.

Zucchini Quiche

| THREE SERVINGS

INGREDIENTS

- 4 pounds (2kg) zucchini
- 2 ounces (50g) yellow cheese, grated
- 7 ounces (200g) 5% feta cheese
- 10 ounces (250g) 5% cottage cheese
- 3 eggs
- Salt and pepper to taste

PREPARATION

1. Cut the zucchini into thin slices. Peeling is not necessary.
2. Cook sliced zucchini with a cup of boiling water until it softens (not more than three minutes after water has boiled again).
3. Because water content in zucchini is high, allow the zucchini to drain thoroughly. Spread the zucchini on three layers of paper towels and squeeze out the excess water.
4. Mix well with cheeses and eggs. Season with salt and pepper.
5. Place in a medium-sized non-stick baking pan. Preheat oven to 375°F (190°C).
6. Bake for 40 minutes or until corners brown. Using a toothpick, check if the quiche is baked thoroughly. You may need to bake for another 10 minutes.

Crispy Steamed Vegetables

| FOUR SERVINGS

INGREDIENTS

- 2 pounds (800g) vegetables
- Salt and pepper to taste

SAUCE

- 2 tablespoons olive oil
- ½ teaspoon balsamic vinegar
- ½ teaspoon salt
- 1 garlic clove, crushed
- Pinch of pepper

ESTIMATED COOKING TIME:

Asparagus, zucchini, and snow peas	Brussel sprouts and carrots	Cauliflower and broccoli	Green beans	Fennel
1 minute	**10 minutes**	**12 minutes**	**14 minutes**	**15 minutes**

PREPARATION

1. Cook vegetables in a small amount of water (1½ cups) for a minimal amount of time in order to retain the vegetables' color, flavor, and nutritional value. Drain water after cooking and remove the pot cover, so that vegetables do not continue to cook in the steam.
2. Cook vegetables separately in order to reach the optimal cooking time for each vegetable. Set a timer for one minute before cooking time is over to ensure vegetables are not overcooked. Check if vegetables are ready by tasting them. They should be tender with a firm appearance. Cook for an additional minute or two if more cooking time is required.
3. Gently coat vegetables evenly in a little dressing to discover and enjoy the vegetables' true taste.

Vegetable & Chickpea Soup

THREE SERVINGS

INGREDIENTS

- 2 onions, diced
- 2 zucchini, cubed
- 1 celery root, cubed
- 1 parsnip, cubed
- 1 cup chickpeas (cooked)
- 1 tablespoon olive oil
- 1 garlic clove, crushed
- 3 cups water
- Salt and pepper to taste

PREPARATION

1. Cook vegetables in water for 20 minutes or until they soften.
2. Season with salt and pepper and add olive oil and garlic.
3. After cooking, add cooked chickpeas.

Optional: Remove half of the cooked vegetables from the pot. Puree the remaining vegetables with an immersion blender. Return vegetable pieces to the pot. Add cooked chickpeas.

Cooked Chickpeas

(ADDITION TO SOUPS AND SALADS)

INGREDIENTS

♡ 1 pound (½ kg) chickpeas (Chickpeas defrost nicely)

PREPARATION

1 Soak chickpeas in a large bowl with half a gallon (2 liters) of water overnight (or for at least 10 hours).
2 Drain the water.
3 Transfer to a pot and cover with water. Bring the water to a boil and cook for one and a half hours on low heat. Check if chickpeas are soft, and cook for another half hour if necessary. Drain the water.
4 Season with ½ teaspoon salt, ¼ teaspoon pepper, and 1 tablespoon olive oil.
5 After cooling, separate into small portions and freeze in Ziploc bags to be served at a later date.

Meeting 5

Private weigh-in

Homework review

The homework last week was to track your mealtimes. Did you learn anything about yourself from this exercise?

What does body fat look like?

Place eight sticks of margarine (2 pounds of fat) and 10 pounds of grocery products in two bags (for example, two packages of flour, two cartons of milk, and 2 pounds of rice) in front of the group.

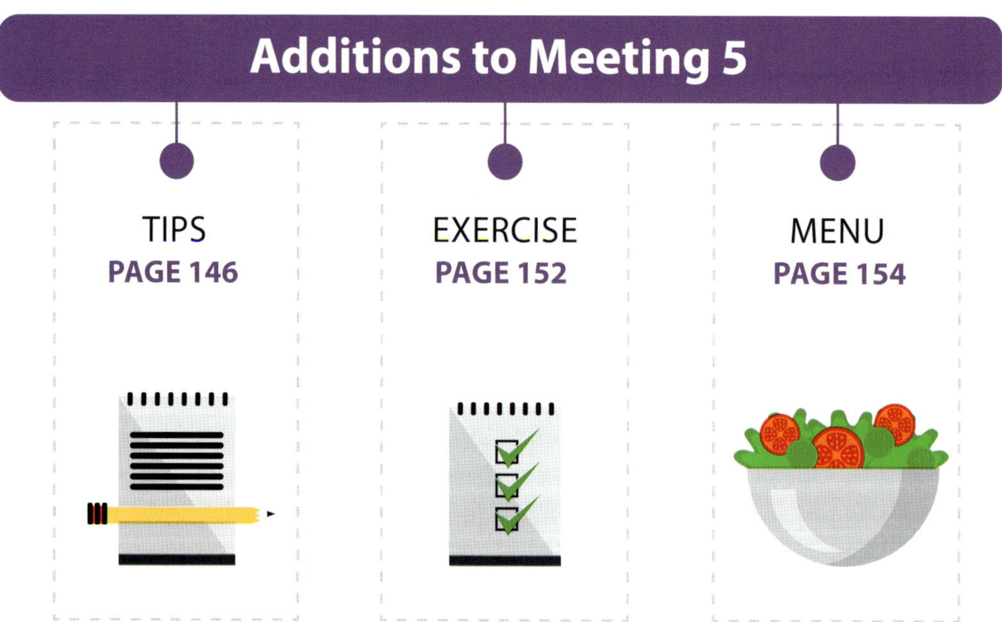

Four weeks into the diet, there is always someone who complains, "I put in so much effort **and I only lost 6 pounds.**" *I want you to understand how much 6 pounds is.*

Look at the 2 pounds of fat – they're very bulky! So when you lose 6 pounds of fat from your body it's quite noticeable. Imagine that you used to have another layer like this around your waist and then you lost it.

Demonstrate by sticking the bars of margarine into pantyhose and wearing them like a belt around your waistline. Everyone will be dying of laughter. Show how easy it is to see the volume of 2 pounds of fat. Then to totally disgust everybody, describe the meat hanging in the refrigerator at the butcher shop.

Layers of white fat that look like margarine are easy to spot. The fat in our bodies also looks like a layer of margarine, as if we were wearing a margarine sweater. Some of this fat enters our veins as well, slowly accumulating there and blocking them.

This fat isn't just bulky – it's also heavy. I want you to feel how heavy 10 pounds are, so I'm going to make each of you go up and down one flight of stairs carrying 10 pounds. You may not have lost 10 pounds yet, but soon everyone here will reach that number.

If there are chairs in the room that weigh about 10 pounds, then have the group pick them up together, for two minutes.

How to give up fattening food forever

This next exercise is very difficult and demands serious effort. It is definitely the most difficult work you'll be asked to do during our meetings. You will need to work hard now, but the benefit will be incredible. Obviously, if you go back to eating all of your old foods after our diet, you'll eventually return to your previous weight. You have to give up some of the foods, forever. Every time we come across a food we gave up for good, we don't ask, "Should I take one or not?" The salivary glands do not secrete saliva. This gets easier with time because there is no decision-making. Everybody knows which foods trigger weight gain. Some of the foods that cause us to gain weight are ones we really like, and others are foods we used to eat senselessly. First, choose to give up these senseless foods. Let me explain what I mean by senseless eating with a personal example. I used to order pizza for the kids for an easy Sunday lunch.

If I were to convince myself that it's not so terrible to eat half a slice of pizza instead of lunch, how many slices would I end up eating? ⌛

At least two! And I don't even like pizza.

Another example of senseless weight gain is that huge box of stale cookies sitting at work. At every meeting, someone brings 20 unappetizing cookies on a few cheap plastic plates.

If I take one cookie, how many will I end up eating? ⌛

Probably 10.

Here we are essentially gaining weight from pure junk by stuffing our body with trans-fat. Another example of gaining weight from junk is eating the kids' leftovers. People commonly gain weight from foods they don't even like. Wafers, for example. If you take a bite of wafer and focus on the taste, you'll notice it's not the most delicious food in the world. But when you open a package, convincing yourself you'll only eat one, of course you'll end up finishing them all.

Think of two foods you are willing to give up forever. Foods that have made you fat and that you prefer to live without. Say the following sentence out loud: "I promise the group I will not eat _______ anymore." Start with something easy and at the next round try to make more of an effort.

Please be honest and don't try to outsmart yourself by giving up something that you don't even eat. Never criticize others. Applaud for other participants who are giving up something really big.

Making this commitment in front of the group really helps. It works like magic. Frequently, I run into people years after they lost weight in my group and they say, "I haven't touched pizza or chocolate chip cookies or peanuts since your group." They tell me this commitment really works because if they gave up eating chocolate, for example, and someone is offering chocolate, they don't start asking themselves if this is good chocolate or not, or whether to take some or not. It's as if the person is offering dog food – it doesn't interest them at all.

I know this commitment is difficult and even scary. I'd like to tell you about a commitment I made in one of my groups. A few years ago, I promised not to eat bagels anymore, and as I made this commitment I was actually shaking, thinking to myself, what will become of me? I didn't know how I would manage the next time we went out to the bagel shop. And what would be left for me to eat? After all, I already banished cake from the house. I promised and shook with fear. This commitment worked like a miracle immediately. The bagels looked bland and stale to me. I thought to myself, who even wants to eat bagels? I learned that it's possible to eat from the salad bar at the bagel shop without any problems.

Introduce this topic at length to ensure the exercise is well understood. It is important!

Who is willing to make this promise to the group and to herself? 

Start with a few volunteers and then move on to those who haven't volunteered yet. If anyone says, "Wow, isn't that too hard?" in response to another participant, I say, "Our job is to encourage fellow participants who make a serious commitment – everyone should focus on her own hard work and decide what she is willing to give up." (Each participant who commits to giving up something big like chocolate deserves a round of applause.)

After every participant has committed to one thing, squeeze another commitment out of them. If someone totally objects, tell her "If you don't give this exercise a try, you will never experience the feeling of freedom and control it brings to your life. You will never experience the magic of making this commitment in front of the group. Suddenly a specific food will not speak to you anymore."

Homework

Tell at least two people about the commitment you made. The more, the better.

Why is it important to tell as many people as possible?

Your commitment doesn't really interest anyone. But you yourself hear what you are saying. The more we speak about the commitment we made, the more we feel obligated to keep it.

Falling in love with salad (It's possible!)

Imagine that you are standing in your kitchen, holding a lemon you took out of the refrigerator. The lemon is cold. Look at the lemon. It is yellowish green and its peel is thin and smooth. Now bring the lemon close to your nose and smell it. It smells great, right? There's nothing like the scent of lemon, right? Next, put the lemon on a cutting board and cut it in half and smell it again. The scent is stronger, right? Now bite into the lemon with your teeth and let the juice run into your mouth.

If you've been following my instructions, your mouth is full of saliva.

Your body reacted to my words and told the salivary glands, "She's biting a lemon, it's sour, secrete saliva to rinse the mouth." In other words, even though there was no actual lemon, the physiological action of secreting saliva from the salivary glands took place. Even simple words running through our minds can affect the salivary glands.

Why is it important to understand the power of our internal monologue? ⌛

The words passing through our minds affect the saliva in our mouths, the secretion of gastric juices, insulin levels, and other bodily processes.

Many of us used to experience something similar when we were children. Remember playing outside with a bunch of friends and hearing your mom call you in for dinner? You are all famished, so you're thrilled that she made everybody's favorite, spaghetti with tomato sauce. You all eat with a hearty appetite until one of the children decides to gross everybody out: "This isn't really spaghetti, it's worms! This red sauce is actually made of cockroaches that Mom found in the grass and put in a bowl. She mashed them up until this red juice came out." One by one, you get disgusted and leave the table without eating.

What happened? Of course, the children know that their mother didn't put mashed cockroaches or worms in the spaghetti. Nevertheless, their thoughts made them nauseous and affected their appetite.

Our physiology is affected by thoughts. Let me give another example:

On Sunday morning, a woman says to herself, "The guests who are coming tonight always give me a headache." Later in the afternoon, she says to herself, "I always get a headache from their noisy kids." As evening arrives, she feels a headache coming on. At 6:00, the guests call to cancel, but their hostess has a headache anyway.

Who caused the headache? The guests or their children? ⌛

Actually, the words going through her mind caused the headache.

If we tell ourselves or others aloud, "I'm sick of these salads already," immediately we generate bodily processes that cause us to reject vegetables. They seem like the worst punishment in the world. Salad begins to disgust us. For us dieters, this is a real catastrophe because we rely on vegetables to be able to lose weight without feeling hungry. When someone says a sentence like this, she might as well take a gun and shoot herself in the foot.

(Pretend to shoot your foot.)

Our goal is to think and speak positively about vegetables and salad. Speaking positively initiates bodily processes that make you crave salad. If you mentally picture a salad with fresh lettuce, nuts, mushrooms, and multicolored cherry tomatoes, topped with fresh-pressed olive oil and croutons, all served in a beautiful bowl, your mouth begins to water and you can't wait to eat the salad. Let's work on this together and entice each other to eat vegetables.

Which vegetables upgrade your salad and turn it into a delicacy? ⌛

Mushrooms, arugula leaves, baby corn, roasted peppers, artichoke hearts...

Homework

Over the next few weeks, on your way home from work, imagine various vegetables and toppings you could add to your salad to make it delicious and different.

Why shouldn't you ever ask yourself, "Do I feel like eating salad?"

Perhaps the answer is no – you're really not in the mood to eat salad. **So you must consider salad a given. You will be eating salad. Now imagine how to turn it into a celebration.** To stimulate salad cravings, it's very helpful to speak at length with positive words about the colorful and wonderful vegetables we have in the world. For example, tell yourself how lucky you are that the carrots are so sweet this season, or how delicious the colorful baby peppers are now.

How can we prompt the body to desire salad even when we don't crave salad?

Even if you don't feel like eating salad, prepare yourself a salad. Start the meal with two bites of salad. These two bites of fresh vegetables will release saliva and gastric juices that will make you crave salad. Incredibly, the first two bites work this magic and our cravings for salad are unlocked.

Learning to control our thoughts

Imagining forbidden foods causes our gastric juices to prepare to eat those harmful foods.

What should you think about instead?

Before any social event, think along these lines: "I will not have any problem with the food. I'll be fine just eating fish and vegetables. It will be so easy and even fun, because I'll see my cousin who I really love and we'll be able to catch up, and I'll drink seltzer with lemon slices in a tall glass with ice cubes that make clinking sounds..." Before going to a social event, think about foods you **can eat**.

If we say, "I will not think about croissants," what will we immediately think about?

Croissants! So when you begin to have thoughts about fattening food, or you're exposed to a conversation or television program about fattening food, physically distance yourself from the conversation or turn off the TV. Occupy yourself with something else that will fill your mind with other thoughts, like planning the next vacation.

Tell yourself out loud and, even more importantly, tell others, "Talking about food used to be one of my hobbies – what was served, what tasted good, and how to make specific dishes. But that doesn't interest me anymore. I have a new hobby now – to be fit and healthy."

Tip: It helps to imagine the nausea and lack of energy you feel after eating

fattening foods – this also affects internal physical processes.

In summary: We can control bodily processes by using our imagination, thoughts, and speech. It's worthwhile to devote our thoughts to pursuing healthy choices.

Homework

Before you fall asleep, imagine your weight-loss success. Instead of thinking about all your worries and not being able to fall asleep, imagine something nice that will calm your mind. Imagining yourself looking and feeling good will affect your behavior. If you imagine this every night of the week, it will be a week when you lose weight!

Imagine the clothing: a small dress, shorts, a tucked in shirt, tight jeans, bathing suit, etc. In your imagination, feel the wonderful sensation of control.

Picture the experience of being thin, the pride and self-confidence. How easy it is to climb stairs, you're practically flying. Feel how you are bursting with energy and joie de vivre.

How to start exercising

Who has been enjoying exercise? Who is willing to share the great feelings and energy that walking brings? ⌛

Even though I said walking is mandatory, there are always participants who do not walk. Sitting on the couch every night thinking "I should be walking now" doesn't help, and it definitely won't get you up and walking. What will get you up and walking? Start by walking a little. Decide that you won't go to sleep until you've walked ten minutes. I know you are totally exhausted after a long day at work, and you don't have the energy to tie your gym shoes let alone leave the house.

You will be surprised at how much energy you'll suddenly have after 20 steps outside. If you consistently walk for ten minutes every day, even after a few days you will feel more energetic throughout the day. You will also sleep better at night and you'll want to walk more. Of course, exercise facilitates weight loss, but it has an additional wonderful benefit – it makes us happier people. Nothing will have changed in your personal life, but nonetheless you will be happier with your life thanks to the added exercise.

Homework

1 Tell at least two people about the foods you promised to give up.

2 Imagine a beautiful salad with tantalizing toppings.

3 Prepare a salad even when you're not in the mood to eat salad.

4 Visualize your weight loss.

5 Discover non-food treats. Come to the next meeting with ideas for how to pamper yourself on a daily basis.

Weekly Exercise

PREPARING A FEEL- GOOD SALAD

Bring the following items for a demonstration: *pre-washed and ready-to-eat lettuce, cabbage, and carrots in a big bowl; a jar of dressing containing 1 tablespoon oil, 1 tablespoon maple syrup, 1 tablespoon lemon juice, 1 tablespoon soy sauce, 2 tablespoons water, 1 crushed garlic clove, ½ teaspoon salt, and a dash of pepper.*

Place the following in small bowls:

- 20 cherry tomatoes
- ½ cup corn kernels
- 3 tablespoons chopped walnuts
- 1 cup cooked chickpeas
- 1 slice of light bread per person

Pass out pencils and the exercise sheet that lists all of the optional salad toppings.

Prepare yourself a salad every day, as the main dish for either lunch or dinner. Today we will learn how to make a feel-good salad – the type that makes you feel good and facilitates weight loss.

First, prepare a big salad with fresh vegetables. Add half a tablespoon of oil from the daily oil allowance and then choose from various enjoyable toppings. Men can choose eight salad toppings for a dietetic meal and woman are permitted six toppings. Write down your ideal salad on the exercise sheet. For example, if you're a woman, you can decide to choose three slices of light bread and 4 ounces (120 g) of chicken.

In front of the group, I demonstrate how to prepare a salad for two women.

How many toppings can be added to a salad for two women? ⌛

12 toppings.

Each woman wants one slice of light bread with the salad, leaving 10 toppings to add. The dressing I prepared contains 1 tablespoon of maple syrup, which counts as one topping and one "free" tablespoon of oil from the daily oil allowance.

How many toppings are left? ⌛

Nine toppings.

Pour the dressing over the salad and toss thoroughly.

Add 3 tablespoons of chopped walnuts (three toppings), 1 cup of chickpeas (four toppings), and ½ cup of corn kernels (two toppings), bringing you to a total of nine toppings.

Give each participant a small bowl of salad, two cherry tomatoes, one slice of light bread, and a plastic fork.

Hand out the weekly menu.

Farewell at the end of the meeting

Don't forget to tell as many people as you can about your promise to give up two foods.

Remember to visualize your weight loss as you fall asleep.

Week 5 Tips

What to bring to Meeting 5

1 | Two packages of margarine (eight sticks) the total should weigh 2 pounds (1 kilo)

2 | Grocery products that weigh a total of 10 pounds (5 kilos)

3 | Exercise sheet for each participant

4 | A big bowl of vegetables and toppings for salad, plus small bowls and forks

5 | Week 5 menu for each participant

6 | Your summary of the meeting's content

7 | Pens or pencils

How to motivate during Week 5

When a participant is standing next to you on the scale, smile at her lovingly. Express excitement even if she has only lost a quarter of a pound (100g). Always say something nice, especially if she didn't lose anything. Offer words of encouragement like "It's only because your body is retaining liquids," "Justice will prevail next week," "Don't give up... keep pushing forward."

How to motivate when a group member complains that she is having a hard time.

I know everything is difficult now and you're asking yourself, "When will this get easier? When will I stop having to control myself all the time? And when will I stop feeling miserable?" I promise that if you persist with eating your feel-good foods for a few month, it will eventually become easier. There will come a time when you go out to a restaurant with friends, and when everybody orders dessert, you'll order a cup of coffee or tea. And miraculously, instead of feeling miserable, you will feel extremely happy. In fact, you will feel like you're bursting with energy and joie de vivre. Decide to make the effort and give this a chance, and you'll see it works.

Extra Topic

ROUND TABLE CONSULTING

Whenever you have free time at the end of the meeting, use it to hold a round table consulting.

A participant brings up a weight-loss-related problem, and the group brainstorms possible solutions together. After this participant finishes explaining her difficulty, each of the other participants gets a turn to say what she would do.

Insist that they always offer their advice in the first person: "I would do the following in this situation." (They can easily slip into saying, "You should do this and that.") No participant, even the one who raised the problem, is allowed to respond. Once the round of advice is over, the participant who raised the problem chooses one thing to implement over the next week. Emphasize that she will not "try" – she will "do." Tell them, "Now, who is ready to be the first to bring up a problem?" Guarantee that the round of advice helps tremendously.

Why does this method of advice-giving help so much?

1 | Being on the receiving end of advice is not always fun. But advice given in the first person softens the message. It's not that everybody is ganging up on her – this same problem also happens to the others.

2 | Allowing the participant to choose what to do from several options makes her feel in control, and the choice obligates her, in front of everybody, to do as she promised.

3 | During this brainstorming process, each participant learns what she could do in a similar situation.

4 | At the end of the discussion, ask the participant to be ready to share how the advice helped at next week's meeting. Receiving feedback and hearing how the discussion solved a participant's problem is extremely rewarding for the entire group.

5 | Sometimes we can solve problems just by listening.

If time allows, the group can discuss two problems.

Homework review

Last week, you were asked to track your mealtimes.

Did you learn anything about yourself from this exercise?

I don't always receive an interesting answer here, but it's important to connect this meeting to the previous one because it creates a feeling that there is follow-up on what they did during the week. To prompt more responses, continue asking them questions. For example, "Did you notice that you were hungrier in the evening on days when you ate a late lunch?"

Learn from my experience

MARGARINE DEMONSTRATION

There is probably no meeting demonstration as impressive as this one. Everyone remembers the margarine. Don't skip it! By the way, margarine keeps in my freezer for years. Etty, one of the group leaders, slid the margarine sticks into sheer nylon pantyhose in a long row, tying the ends around her waist to demonstrate. The margarine goes into the freezer inside this creative attire at the end of the meeting!

HOW TO GIVE UP FATTENING FOOD FOREVER

This exercise is unique to our weight-loss method and is life-altering for participants. I meet people who lost weight in my group 20 years ago and they tell me, "Ever since I made my commitment not to eat peanuts in the group, I haven't even touched one." It works like magic. Also, a common language develops between the participants. When a participant shares that she has a problem with a specific food, someone in the group answers, "Commit for one month," and everyone else knows what she's talking about.

Try to have every participant make at least one small promise that allows her to experience the power of making a commitment.

Take into account that some people don't want to make this commitment, and to avoid it, they make noise or even sabotage other participants' commitments. Tell everyone to be quiet and concentrate primarily on their own hard work.

It's definitely worth bearing in mind an incident that happened in one of my groups. A really sweet woman in the group lost weight nicely up until this exercise. As I introduced the exercise of committing to give up specific foods, she repeatedly interrupted me, saying "I will not give up chocolate." As expected, all those announcements about chocolate caused her to go home and eat chocolate – apparently lots of chocolate, because at the next weigh-in she had gained a great deal of weight.

Since this incident, whenever a participant begins to tell me what she is unwilling to give up, I ask her not to focus on it, telling her, "If you focus on the foods you are unwilling to give up, you will go home and eat them and ruin the weight-loss process. Concentrate on the foods that make you gain weight that you are willing to give up."

INSPIRATIONAL STORIES

Beginning the following week, at the sixth meeting, I start each meeting with inspirational stories from participants. I ask each participant to prepare a story for next week about a difficult situation (related to the diet) and how she heroically succeeded.

ASK MEMBERS TO GIVE YOU CREDIT

This week is the right time to take two minutes from the meeting for your public relations.

Ask members to give you credit: "If someone asks you how you lost weight, please answer: in the Kosloff method group. If you answer that you changed your eating habits, you will not send me the next customer and you will not help the person that asked the question."

Story Time

SHARON DIDN'T NOTICE THAT SHE ATE A TON

Two sisters once joined one of my groups. Emily was very enthusiastic, and wanted to lose about 15 pounds, while her sister, Sharon, was heavy, clumsy, and at least 60 pounds overweight. Emily lost weight at an excellent pace, and Sharon didn't lose weight at all. When I asked Sharon how the past week went, she answered that she had followed the diet perfectly, adding that apparently this diet didn't suit her.

One week, Sharon didn't attend the meeting. Emily approached me and said, "Listen, obviously Sharon is eating many more calories than the menu allows and doesn't even notice." She continued to tell me the following story: "Last week, my sister and I attended an afternoon wedding. I filled a big plate up with salads and said 'this is what I'm eating for lunch.' Sharon didn't like that idea at all and said that the salads were too fattening, full of oil, nuts, and high-fat cheese, and that she planned to eat at home." As they chitchatted at the table, Emily watched her sister reach for one French fry after another, until she slowly finished an entire bowl of French fries all by herself. After the wedding, Emily suggested they go to the mall together, but Sharon said, "You are full because you ate a ton, but I'm starving because I didn't eat a thing. I can't wait to go home and eat." To make a long story short, Sharon didn't notice that she ate a ton – many more calories than Emily did. She could have sworn that she hadn't eaten anything.

Even if you suspect the participant didn't follow the menu, never insinuate that she is being dishonest.

If a participant hasn't lost weight for two weeks, ask her to write down everything she eats during the week and bring it to the next meeting. Make a note on her personal card that you asked her to keep a log. At the next meeting, ask her for the log, and call her during the week to discuss it. Many times, participants lose weight nicely when they keep a log. Alternatively, ask her to take a picture of everything she eats and send it to you by WhatsApp. If she forgets to send a picture of her breakfast the next morning, send her a short message: "Breakfast?"

Week 5 Exercise

PREPARING A FEEL-GOOD SALAD

Eating salad every day for lunch provides countless benefits. This satisfying meal leaves you feeling energetic for the rest of the day and not drowsy post-meal. It's super easy to prepare a refreshing salad at home or at work.

Step 1

Prepare a large vegetable salad including a minimum of 3 cups of fresh vegetables.

Step 2

Add your favorite dressing.
"Free" dressing options: half of the daily oil allowance, mustard, fresh lemon juice, balsamic vinegar, soy sauce, crushed garlic, grated ginger, lemon zest, oregano, water, salt, and pepper.

Step 3

Treat yourself to delicious and healthy toppings.
For women: 6 toppings
For men, athletes, and breastfeeding mothers: 8 toppings

How can you upgrade your salad even more?

♥

Buy a beautifully designed salad bowl.

Salad toppings

1 slice of light bread

1 tablespoon tahini sauce or 1 teaspoon oil

½ hard-boiled egg

1.5 ounces (40g) 5% fat feta cheese

½ apple or ½ pear or ½ orange

½ small avocado

1 tablespoon of sesame seeds or ground nuts or sunflower seeds

1.5 ounces (40g) chicken breast or cold cuts

¼ cup corn kernels

1.5 ounces (40g) tuna, drained of oil

1 tablespoon cranberries or raisins

1 tablespoon of dates syrup or honey or maple syrup

¼ cup cooked chickpeas

4 large olives or 8 small olives

Week 5 Menu

TREAT YOURSELF WITH A FEEL-GOOD SALAD.
IMAGINE YOURSELF THINNER

sport

DAY 1

BREAKFAST	♡ Beverage: coffee, tea, water ♡ 2 slices of light bread ♡ 2 tablespoons 5% low-fat cottage cheese ♡ Tomato and cucumber slices
10:00 AM	♡ Beverage: coffee, tea, water ♡ 10 walnuts halves and vegetable sticks
LUNCH	♡ Beverage: coffee, tea, water ♡ Five-color Salad ♡ 5 ounces (150g) of chicken or fish ♡ 1 slice of light bread
16:00 PM	♡ Beverage and apple
DINNER	♡ Beverage: coffee, tea, water ♡ 3 tablespoons tahini sauce (or 1 tablespoons raw tahini) ♡ Oven-baked Vegetables (recipe included) ♡ 2 slices of light bread ♡ Cucumber slices

♥ Snack on fresh vegetable sticks and cherry tomatoes between meals ♥ Eat up to 2 cups of vegetable soup per day ♥ Lunch and dinner can be switched ♥ Drink beverages without added milk or sugar ♥ Eat at least 2 cups of vegetables at lunch and again at dinner ♥ One tablespoon of oil per day is mandatory ♥

DAYS 2, 3, 4		sport
BREAKFAST	Beverage: coffee, tea, water	
	1 slice of light bread	
	2 tablespoons avocado	
	Vegetable sticks	
10:00 AM	Beverage and yogurt	
LUNCH	Beverage: coffee, tea, water	
	Five-color Salad + 15 cashews	
	3.5 ounces (100g) tofu (recipe included) or 3.5 ounces (100g) of another protein	
16:00 PM	Beverage and apple	
DINNER	Beverage: coffee, tea, water	
	3.5 ounces (100g) fish or chicken	
	Stir-fried Vegetables (recipe included)	
	1 slice of light bread	

DAYS 5, 6, 7		sport
BREAKFAST	Beverage: coffee, tea, water	
	1 slice of light bread	
	3 tablespoons 2% low-fat cottage cheese	
	Tomato and cucumber slices	
10:00 AM	Beverage and yogurt	
LUNCH	Beverage: coffee, tea, water	
	Israeli Salad (recipe included)	
16:00 PM	Beverage and apple	
DINNER	Beverage: coffee, tea, water	
	Moussaka (recipe included)	
	Five-color Salad	

Recipes

Oven-roasted Vegetables

THREE SERVINGS

This is my favorite - it is soooo tasty. I bake a variety of vegetables in the largest pan that fits in the oven. I don't put salt, pepper, oil, or other seasoning and I don't peel the vegetables.

The preparation takes just five minutes, which keeps me in the habit of making this dish every week.

When the vegetables are ready you can eat them with 3 tablespoons of tahini and two slices of light bread as a full meal. You can replace the tahini with 2 tablespoons of meat sauce or pasta sauce. The baked veggies are a delicious substitute for pasta.

INGREDIENTS

- ♡ 1 cauliflower, divided into 2-inch florets
- ♡ 1 eggplant, unpeeled, cut in half or quarters depending on the size
- ♡ 2 large red peppers, whole
- ♡ 2 zucchini, cut in to rounds
- ♡ 2 fennel, cut into 3 pieces
- ♡ 2 red onions, cut into quarters (not pulled apart)

***This is a recommended list. Select four of the listed vegetables to roast, according to your preference.**

PREPARATION

1. Line a baking pan with baking paper.
2. Separate the cauliflower into 2-inch florets.
3. Slice the eggplant in half and place on the pan, skin side down.
4. Place the onions, fennel, peppers, and zucchini on the baking pan.
5. Insert the baking pan into a pre-heated 375°F (190°C) oven. Bake for 40 minutes.
6. Remove the peppers and place in a closed Tupperware container. They will be easier to peel after they cool.
7. Leave the remaining vegetables in the oven for another 10-15 minutes, until the cauliflower and eggplant are slightly brown.

Tahini Sauce

You can find tahini paste at some specialty Mediterranean and Middle Eastern stores, but many grocers are starting to carry tahini paste. Choose a tahini paste that is made of 100% sesame seeds with nothing else.

INGREDIENTS

- 4 tablespoons tahini paste
- 1 minced garlic clove
- ¼ teaspoon salt, pinch of pepper
- 2 tablespoons lemon juice
- 2-4 tablespoons water
- 1 tablespoon parsley, finely diced.

PREPARATION

Put the tahini in small bowl, add the garlic, salt and pepper.

Add the lemon juice and stir until the lemon juice is all blended. Add the water one tablespoon at a time, and continue to stir. At a certain point of adding fluid the tahini texture will change from creamy to a strange consistency. Don't get scared, continue to stir and add water until it will look creamy again. Add garlic, salt and pepper. When serving, add fresh parsley on top.

You can keep this sauce in the fridge in a tightly closed plastic box for 3 days.

Ruthy's Tofu (four servings)

Ruthy says this is the best tofu recipe ever! Even her kids are crazy about it!

| FOUR SERVINGS

INGREDIENTS

- 1 pound (400g) tofu, cubed

SAUCE

- ½ cup of parsley, chopped
- 1 tablespoon crushed ginger
- 1 teaspoon olive oil
- 2 tablespoons soy sauce
- Salt and pepper to taste

PREPARATION

1. Cut tofu into ½-inch cubes and marinate in the sauce for half an hour. Mix tofu in the marinade a few times.
2. Line a large baking pan with baking paper, scatter the tofu cubes and marinade on the pan, and bake for 15 minutes until it browns.

***Use fresh ginger. Wrap a ginger root in plastic and store in the freezer. Grate the desired amount while the ginger is still frozen, then return to the freezer.**

Stir-fried Vegetables

THREE SERVINGS

INGREDIENTS

- 2 tablespoons oil
- 2 onions, chopped
- 1 whole cabbage, shredded
- 2 pounds (1kg) zucchini, sliced
- 2 red onions, quartered, not pulled apart
- 3 tablespoons soy sauce

PREPARATION

1. In a very large saucepan, stir-fry two onions in 2 tablespoons oil until browned.
2. Add red onion.
3. Add shredded cabbage and continue to mix.
4. Cook until the cabbage becomes translucent, then add zucchini.
5. Add soy sauce and continue cooking on low heat for another three minutes until zucchini softens.

Israeli Salad

ONE SERVING

INGREDIENTS

- 1 hard-boiled egg
- ¼ cup cooked chickpeas
- 2 medium size tomatoes
- 3 small cucumbers
- ½ small red onion
- 1 tablespoon parsley

SAUCE

- 2 tablespoon tahini sauce

PREPARATION

Finely dice tomatoes, cucumbers, onion and parsley. Add tahini sauce just before serving.

Add the chickpeas on the side of the dish. Cut the hard-boiled egg to four pieces and decorate the dish with them

Moussaka

FOUR SERVINGS

INGREDIENTS

- 1 pound (500g) lean ground meat
- 3 eggplants, cut into ¾-inch (2 cm) rounds
- 2 zucchini, grated
- 1 garlic clove, crushed
- 2 onions, chopped
- 1 tablespoon oil
- 1 carrot, grated
- Parsley, chopped

SAUCE

- 1 egg
- 1 cup tomatoes, diced (fresh or canned)
- 2 garlic cloves, crushed
- Salt and pepper to taste

PREPARATION

1. Place eggplant on a baking pan lined with baking paper. Insert the baking pan into pre-heated 375°F (190°) oven. Bake for half an hour or until eggplant browns.
2. Taste a small piece of eggplant to check that it is ready to eat at this stage. If not, return to oven and bake for longer. Pay attention!! It is essential that eggplant is ready to eat before you fill it with meat.
3. While eggplant is baking, sauté onion in a skillet. After the onion becomes translucent, add carrots for three minutes, and then add meat.
4. Brown meat and add grated zucchini for another four minutes.
5. After cooking, add parsley, garlic, and seasonings. Heat together until boiling, then turn off flame.
6. Layer eggplant and meat alternately in a large 9 x 13 Pyrex dish, starting with meat and ending with eggplant.
7. Mix sauce well and pour over the top.
8. Bake in a pre-heated 375°F (190°C) oven for half an hour, or until sauce browns.

Appendix

How to start your first weight-loss group

One of the greatest things about leading weight-loss groups is that every participant who loses twenty pounds or more becomes a walking billboard advertising your group. Everyone asks them how they did it and just like that new members flock to you.

But how can you get started?

1 | Set the group's starting date one month out. Pick a day, time, and location. If the first group is small, you can conduct the meetings at your home or at the home of one of the participants. Tell everyone you meet about the new weight-loss group starting soon.

Express complete confidence that the group will start on the set day and time and at the set price.

2 | If someone tells you she may be interested and needs to think about it, write down her name and telephone number in a **notebook** you've prepared ahead of time for this opportunity. Likewise, if a friend says that her sister may be interested, write down "Renee's sister is possibly interested" and include Renee's phone number. Two weeks before the starting date, call all of the people you wrote down in the notebook.

3 | Hang up a **small flyer** at the local hairdresser's, supermarket, and neighborhood community center.

4 | Three weeks before the group is scheduled to begin, **make 100 photocopies of the flyer** and distribute them to your neighbors' mailboxes. At the top of the flyer, write "Here on Chestnut Road." The flyer should include your full name – it doesn't make a good impression if you leave it out.

5 | Facebook, WhatsApp, other social networking sites, email lists, local newspapers, and the community center's journal are all great places to advertise without spending too much money.

6 | Two weeks before the starting date, call each of your acquaintances to tell them about the weight-loss group you are leading and ask them to help you to spread the word. Mention that you're offering the group at a special price so people can get to know you. Be enthusiastic about the first meeting, assuring them it will be interesting, useful, and free.

7 | The best way to start is also the simplest – invite over a few friends who want to lose weight and start the program. The biggest secret to leading weight-loss groups is to start the first group even if there are only two participants.

How can you build a successful support group?

☺ With lots of support!!!

The leader plays a vital part in the weight-loss journey. She is there to lend support with phone calls, text messages, e-mails, and the WhatsApp and Facebook groups. Calling participants regularly and encouraging them to call whether they're struggling or just want some advice about a recipe makes them feel taken care of. Small gifts are also a valuable tool for motivating participants throughout the process. Most importantly, however, the leader must ensure that the group focuses only on topics, activities, and behaviors conducive to weight-loss.

A small and supportive group allows participants to get acquainted and encourage each other. For this reason, no new participants may join after the first meeting. Each participant feels like she is contributing to the group by sharing ideas and recipes, offering encouragement, and helping in activities like the salad workshop.

Our supportive menu plan is healthy, easy to prepare, and, best of all, can be maintained long-term. The menu is a wonderful guide to developing healthy eating habits for life.

THE KOSLOFF METHOD IS BASED ON GUIDELINES THAT HELP CREATE A SUCCESSFUL GROUP:

1 | After the first trial week, participants commit to participating in meetings and investing effort long-term, in addition to their financial commitment. This method eliminates all those who are not ready to work hard. If these people remain in the group, they may interfere with the other participants' progress.

2 | We speak about successes and victories and we don't let participants share stories about failures.

3 | The number of participants should not exceed 25. A group this size allows members to become well acquainted, and group discussion rounds are easier to conduct.

4 | The group meets for at least six months. Someone recovering from years of poor eating habits needs to be in a weight-loss program for a long period of time in order to make a permanent lifestyle change.

5 | The program includes exercises that change participants' way of thinking by revealing their negative thought patterns about food and eating habits. Subsequently, participants learn how to reverse negative thinking for good.

How to adapt the menu for members who need more calories

The menus in this book include 1200 calories per day. Men, women who weigh over 250 pounds (120 kg), and anyone who exercises more than an hour and a half per day all need to add 300 calories to their daily menu.

HOW TO CHANGE OUR MENU TO INCLUDE 1500 CALORIES

Add **all** three of the following items:

AN ADDITIONAL TABLESPOON OF OIL.

AN ADDITIONAL LIGHT MEAL:
AN APPLE, YOGURT, OR SANDWICH OR 12 ALMONDS

AN ADDITIONAL 3.5 OUNCES (100 GR.) OF PROTEIN AT ONE OF THE MEALS: WHITE SOFT CHEESE, FISH, CHICKEN (UNCOOKED).

NURSING MOTHERS

Nursing mothers are given the 1500-calorie menu plan plus an additional 300 calories, for a total of 1800 calories per day. Dairy products, such as cheeses, yogurt, and milk are highly recommended for nursing mothers. Even though nursing mothers eat many more calories per day, they tend to lose weight faster than the rest of us.

How to adapt the menu for vegetarians

YOU CAN HAVE AN ADDITIONAL TABLESPOON OF OIL EACH DAY, TO BE EATEN WITH VEGETABLES.

YOU CAN REPLACE ANY MEAT PORTION IN LUNCH OR DINNER WITH ONE OF THE FOLLOWING PORTIONS:

Soy products like cutlets or tofu, up to 200 calories

OR 7 ounces (200 g) 5% fat soft white cheese

OR 5 ounces (150 g) 5% feta cheese

OR 2 eggs + 5 olives

How to adapt the menu for people who don't eat dairy products

You can replace 1 tablespoon of cheese with any of the following:

1 tablespoon avocado

OR 1 teaspoon hummus/ tahini/ canned tuna fish

OR 1 slice pastrami

Whenever the menu calls for cheese by weight you may substitute fish or chicken of the same weight.

The secret contract between the group leader and participants

Many years ago, during one of the groups I led, I did the unacceptable.

At the fifth meeting, I asked the participants if anyone objected to moving the meetings to another day. Everyone agreed, except for one woman. I went ahead and changed the meeting to a different day of the week. This woman, who couldn't continue with the group, called me later and explained why what I did was so terrible. She claimed that even though certain things were never explicitly said or written, and we had never signed a contract of any sort, unwritten rules exist between the group leader and participants. She was totally right. When you start a group, the details you decide on and notify the participants of are as much of an obligation as a contract. In these unwritten rules, it is explicitly said that the customer pays to join a weight-loss group for period of time and receives the following in return:

Upon starting a group, the leader sets the price, day, time, and location and must stick to those terms. (The location can be moved to another place in the same neighborhood.)

The leader may not go on vacation or cancel a meeting for the entire time period paid in advance. (After 10 meetings, it is okay to take a short vacation and skip one meeting.)

Weight loss is the only topic of conversation. The leader is a superhero. The group relates to her respectfully, affectionately, and with a certain sense of awe. So when she rambles on about something unrelated to weight loss, participants listen attentively. Oddly, they also know to laugh at all the right times and nobody dares to get annoyed or comment.

But in reality, the participants are angry.

Years ago I participated in an exercise class. The instructor cancelled a class because she was travelling abroad and didn't bother to find a substitute.

At the next class, she took fifteen minutes of our time to tell us about how she was detained at customs.

That was the last time I came to this instructor's exercise class. I never said anything to her and she probably didn't even know I was angry that she had wasted my time after I paid for both the class and a babysitter. It was really annoying, and I had no desire to see her again.

Frequently there is something interesting in the news or one of the participants is excited about a particular event. It is the leader's role to quiet any unrelated chatter and to remind the participants again and again that the group only discusses weight loss. In the event that someone starts to speak about an unrelated topic, I just say "Let's get back to our topic…"

The leader must be prepared for the lecture. When I conduct a training course for group leaders, I film them practicing the first meeting in my living room. Afterwards, we watch the video together. I recommend that you also film yourself practicing the first meeting and then watch the video. Do you notice how beautiful you look when you smile? Does your smile make members feel like they're in good hands? Are your hand motions interesting and engaging? Did you radiate confidence that participants will succeed on this weight-loss journey?

The meeting's content will be summarized by chapter titles. To generate interest, make eye contact with the participants as you speak. During the meeting, the leader should never be busy with the class syllabus and should definitely never read straight from the book or handouts.

To remind yourself which topics should be discussed during the meeting, summarize each in one or two sentences and print the sentences in large letters on a piece of paper or on index cards.

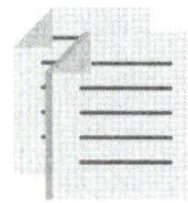

All handouts should be ready at the meeting. At each meeting, the leader hands out menu sheets, reading material, and exercise sheets. Prepare the sheets a few meetings in advance. Speaking from experience, I know that many problems crop up when you're photocopying papers and they always arise when you decide to photocopy half an hour before the meeting.

Respectful and professional attire. I highly recommend dressing nicely for the meeting. Before buying any article of clothing, I look in the store's mirror and ask myself, "Is this appropriate for delivering a lecture?" If the answer is no, I don't buy it.

Accurate scale. Once you have 20 participants, it's worthwhile to purchase a professional scale. If you are leading a small group, a reliable home scale is sufficient. How to test for reliability? Get on and off the scale five times, leaning more on one foot, then more on the other. The scale must show the same weight each time. A deviation of 0.2 pound (100 gr.) between each weighing is acceptable.

Closed group. Believe me – I know how tempting it is to add one more participant. After you have already met twice, someone calls and begs to join the group. Do not be tempted to let her join because you will lose both your exclusivity and your group's special intimacy.

This is the contract that exists between you and each participant, and these are the unwritten rules you must absolutely follow. And what do you receive in return?

The tremendous satisfaction of watching participants make the changes they desire, all because of you.

How to print the exercises and menus – in a printer-friendly version and for free!

Please go to **www.ykosloff.com/book** to register, and you'll get a link to the pdf versions of the exercises and menus via email.

How to continue now that the first five meetings have come and gone

I have found that in order to make a significant change in life, such as leaving bad eating habits behind and developing good ones, a person must participate in a group for at least half a year. Therefore, dear leader, please continue with the meetings, beyond the five meetings included in this book. You can be creative and develop your own class syllabi of additional meetings for the group you've started. Each meeting someone from the group can bring a printed vegetable recipe for everyone, and so on....

I am now working on another book that will have additional meetings and menus. But in the meantime, if you would like to buy a pdf version of meetings and menus 6-9, please go to **www.ykosloff.com/book2**

Epilogue

Yesterday I felt depressed, exhausted, and drained of energy. I left the house to lead a group meeting and, like always, a transformation occurred: the positive energy and the group's warm embrace erased my bad mood and I returned home happy and energetic.

Thank you to the thousands of people who have participated in my groups, bringing me happiness and making me feel I have meaning in this world. Many participants have made valuable contributions to the syllabus content during group meetings. Thank you as well for this.

Thank you to the Kosloff Method leaders – each and every one of you contributed to this book in your own unique way.

Thanks to my cousin, Bruria Hurvits, for looking over the Hebrew manuscript and correcting many errors.

Thank you to my dear friend, Avital Bar, for contributing greatly to the book's structure. Thank you to Aliza Nadav for your excellent translation. Thanks to Taylor Johnston for editing the English version.

Thank you to Miriam Navot for her valuable remarks on the book.

Thank you to everyone who believed in me and encouraged me to continue writing during the long periods of time when I was feeling stuck: my husband, Ronnie Kosloff; my children, Omri Kedem, Aviv Kosloff, and Elad Kosloff; my close friends, Jeff and Yochi Gordon; and my friend Moshe Heller, who is both my neighbor and publisher.

I especially wish to thank the incredible designer, Maya Enov, for this book's beautiful design. Maya lost weight through the Kosloff Method and significantly contributed to this book. Without her close and loving support, as well as our weekly meetings in my kitchen, this book would not have been possible.

I love you all,

Yaffa Kosloff

Notes